Black Historical Figures

HBCUs

Copyright © 2022 by Every Dollar Countz LLC
All rights reserved. This book or any portion thereof
may not be reproduced or used in any manner whatsoever
without the express written permission of the publisher
except for the use of brief quotations in a book review.

TABLE OF CONTENTS

107 JACKSON STATE

179 MORGAN STATE

11 CENTRAL STATE

3	Spelman	67	Morehouse	131	Fisk
11	Central State	75	Southern	139	Maryland Eastern Shore
19	Howard	83	Tuskegee	147	Claflin
27	Alcorn State	91	Norfolk	155	Winston Salem
35	Xavier of Louisiana	99	Florida AM	163	Delaware State
43	Elizabeth	107	Jackson State	171	Tougaloo
51	Hampton	115	North Carolina A&T	179	Morgan State
59	Alabama State	123	Clark Atlanta	187	Dillard
				195	North Carolina Central

These Workbooks are geared to intrigue, inspire and motivate you to want to learn more about these Black Historical Figures(BHFs) and others. Also to do more research on your own. We know this isn't all the history of these individuals. We want you to do some of the research also. We try to be as accurate as possible during our research. If there are some stories or questions that aren't as stated, please contact us at info@wegonnalearntoday.com.

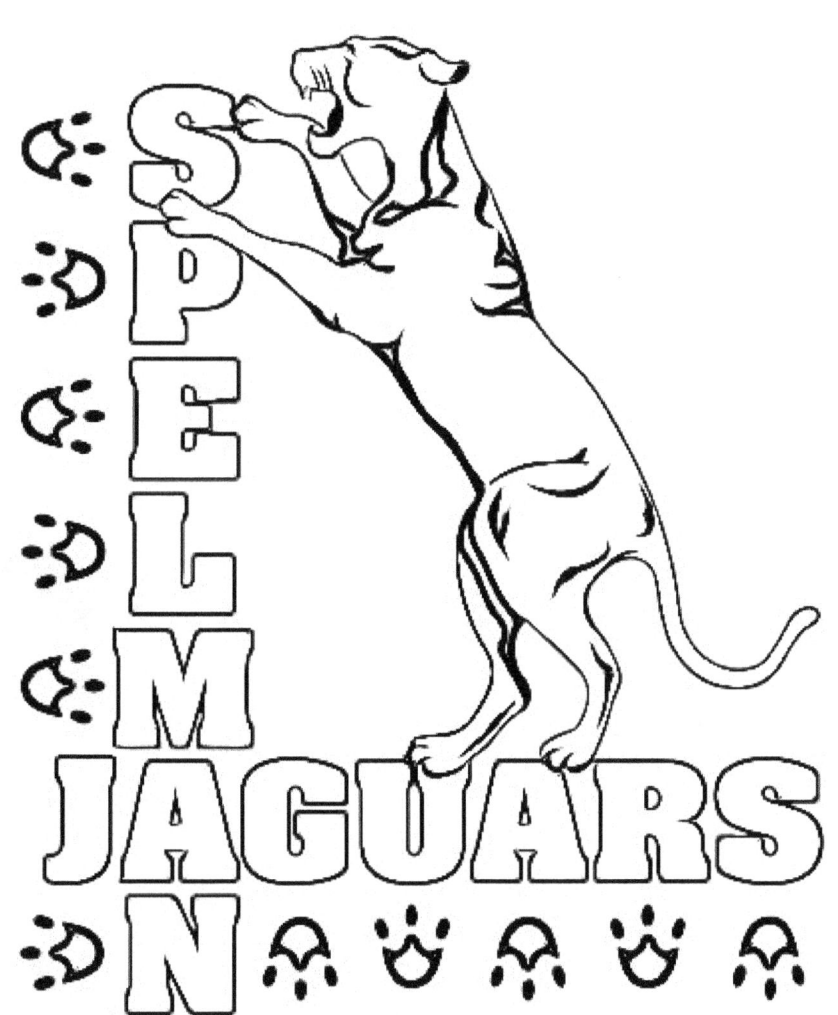

APRIL 11, 1881 – PRESENT

LEFT BLANK ON PURPOSE

Spelman College

Spelman College

Spelman College

Spelman College

Spelman College

Spelman College

Directions: read the bio below and answer the following questions.

Atlanta Baptist Female Seminary, which is now called Spelman College, is a private women's HBCU that is dedicated to academic excellence in the liberal arts and sciences, as well as the intellectual, creative, ethical and leadership development of its students. It was founded on April 11, 1881, in Atlanta, GA, in the basement of Friendship Baptist Church by two teachers from the Oread Institute of Worcester, MA: Harriet E. Giles and Sophia B. Packard. In 1884, John D. Rockefeller visited the school. He was so impressed that he settled the debt on the property. Rockefeller's wife, Laura Spelman Rockefeller, her sister, Lucy Spelman and their parents, Harvey Buel and Lucy Henry Spelman, were also supportive of the school. The Spelmans were longtime activists in the abolitionist movement. In 1884, the name of the school was changed to the Spelman Seminary in honor of Laura Spelman and her parents. In 1924, the school became Spelman College.

1. Where was Spelman founded at?
   A. Worcester, MA
   B. Atlanta, GA
   C. Richford, NY
2. What was our name prior to 1884?
   A. Spelman College
   B. Atlanta Baptist Female Seminary
   C. Spelman Seminary
3. Who is Spelman College named after?
   A. Harriet E. Giles's mother
   B. John D. Rockefeller's wife
   C. Sophia B. Packard's mother

Directions: Answer the questions to solve the crossword puzzle. You can use the internet if you get stuck on any question.

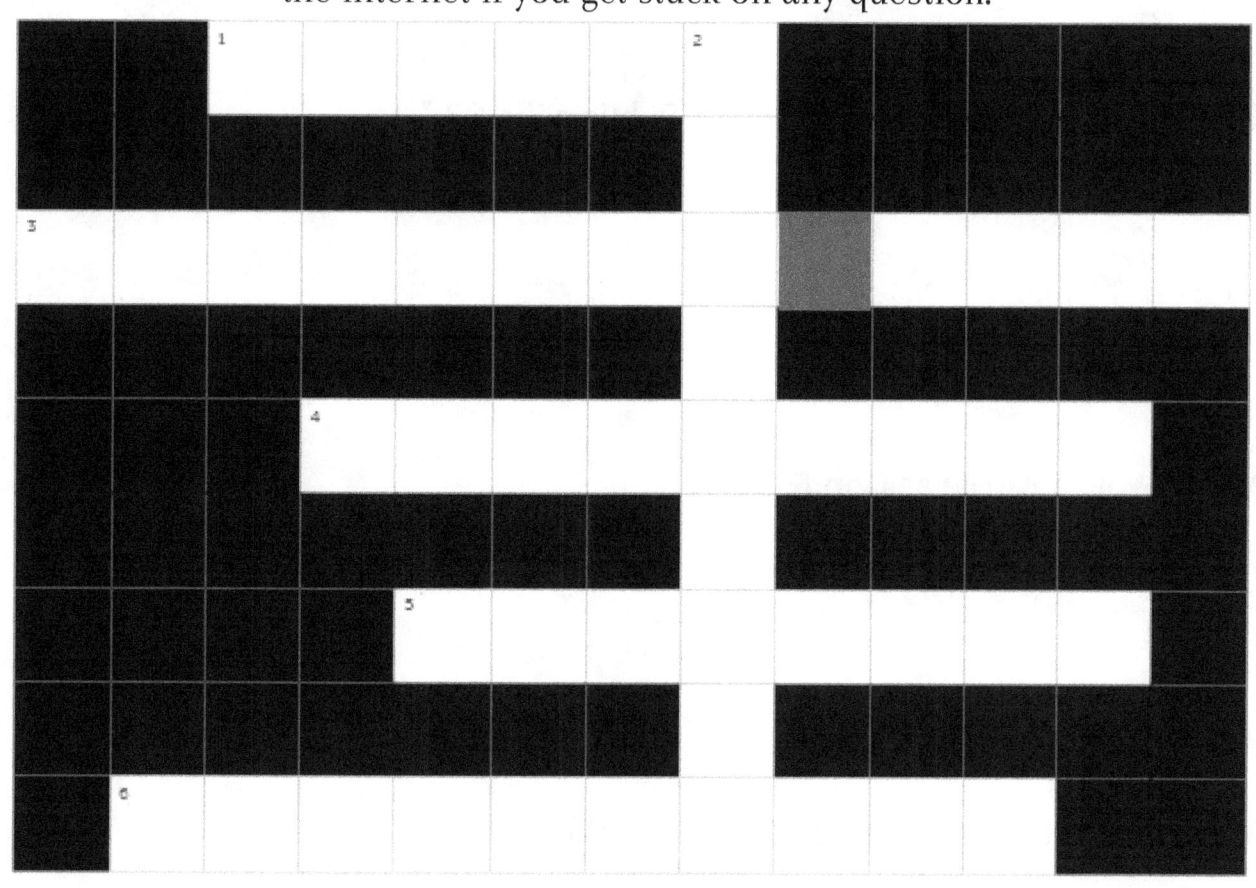

Across
1) Spelman's motto is "Our Whole School for ____."
3) Spelman's school colors are ____ and white.
4) Johnnetta Betsch Cole was elected as the first Black woman ____ of Spelman College.
5) Spelman began in 1881 as the Atlanta Baptist Female ____.
6) Spelman's Nora Gordon is the first student to become a ____ to Africa.

Down
2) Spelman's has a ____ were Spelmanites wearing "respectable and conservative" white attire to designated formal events on campus.

Directions: Read and answer the questions. These are your opinions so the answers will vary.

Would you rather go to a HBCU or a Public college?

What's your favorite season & why?

What career are you most interested in? Why?

Directions: Unscramble the words below about Spelman. See if you can get the bonus word.

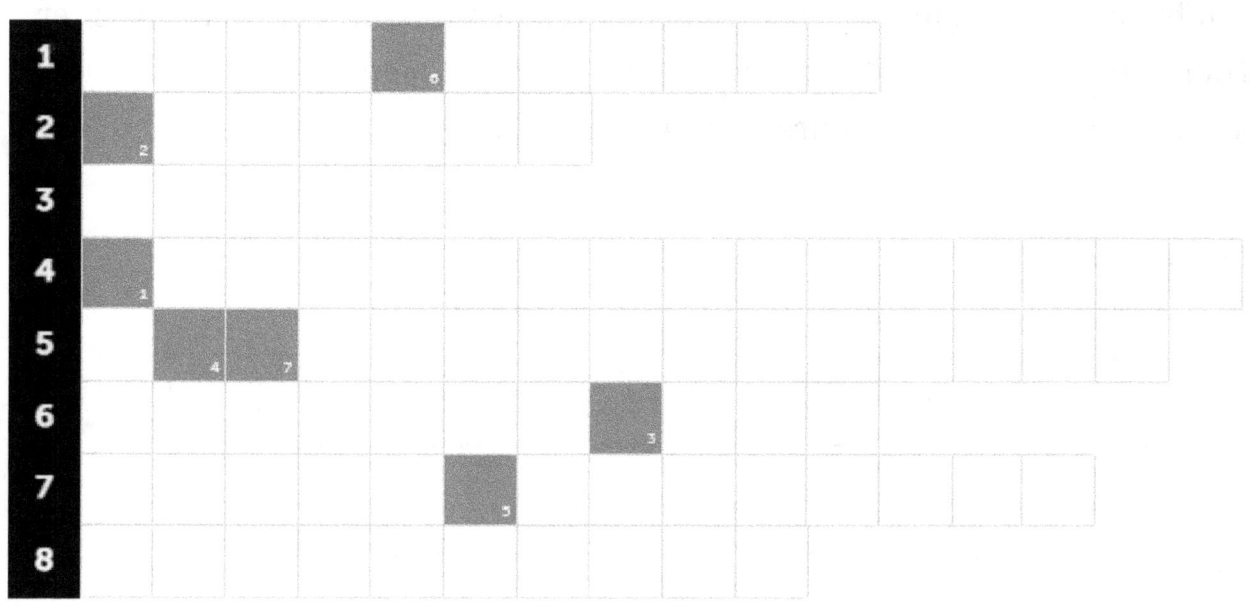

BONUS WORD

Unscramble Words

1) alrrilatebs
2) taantla
3) nmeow
4) cjehledoroknfler
5) nsemteuarmfuiof
6) gtcrvilsiih
7) proakscpiabadh
8) odziannwrh

Directions: This is the WGLT Challenge. Solve the cryptogram. As the puzzle solver, you need to find which number belongs to which character. And this can be pretty challenging! You will need to match the number with the letter. There are some letters given to you below. This will help you solve the other words and unlock more characters. **Good Luck.**

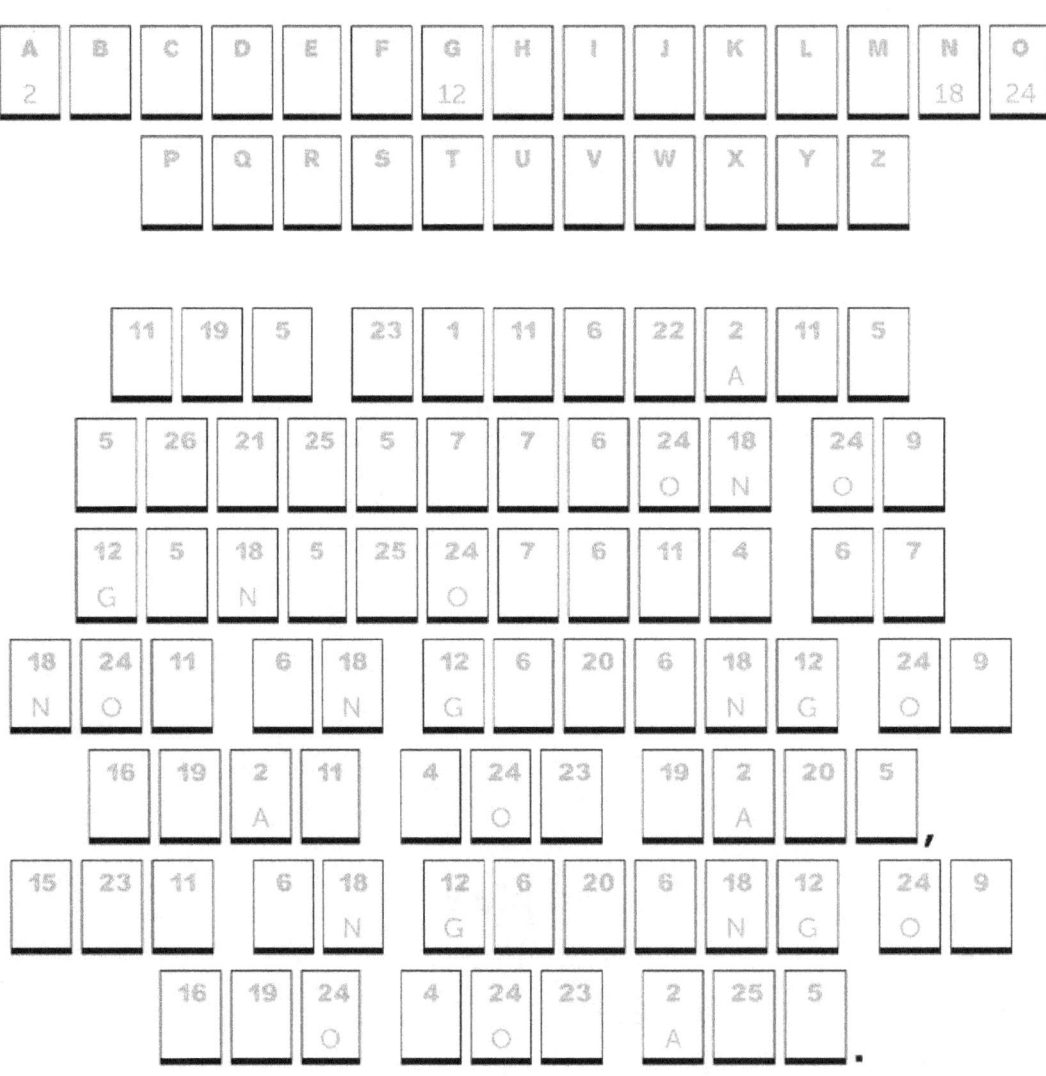

Central State

University

Central State

University

1887 – PRESENT

LEFT BLANK ON PURPOSE

Central State

University

Central State

University

Directions: read the bio below and answer the following questions.

The Combined Normal and Industrial Department, which is now called Central State University (CSU), is a public historically Black land-grant university that prepares students with diverse backgrounds and experiences for leadership, research and service. Established by the state legislature in 1887 in Wilberforce, OH, the school was originally located at Wilberforce University, which is a private HBCU in Wilberforce, OH. Affiliated with the African Methodist Episcopal Church (AME), this college was the first college to be owned and operated by African Americans. In 1941, the department expanded from a two-year to a four-year program and in 1947, it legally split from Wilberforce and became the College of Education and Industrial Arts at Wilberforce. In 1951, the college changed their name to Central State College. With further development, the college gained university status in 1965. In 2014, Central State University was designated a land-grant university.

1. How did CSU come to be a college?
    A. Wilberforce University created a new department
    B. AME created a new college
    C. State legislation was enacted
2. What year did Wilberforce become a college?
    A. 1947
    B. 1951
    C. 1941
3. What is special about Wilberforce University?
    A. It's the first college that was owned and operated by African-Americans
    B. They started Central State University
    C. They provide classical education

Directions: Find the words associated with Central State.

U	M	A	E	W	I	L	B	E	R	F	O	R	C	E	B	B	T
W	K	I	G	R	D	U	D	G	U	I	S	Y	V	Z	A	W	H
R	B	R	J	K	W	P	C	N	Z	F	N	C	K	H	M	W	M
E	R	D	L	O	G	D	N	A	N	O	O	R	A	M	E	H	P
K	A	U	M	C	Y	L	F	C	H	Z	I	S	K	M	-	K	F
E	W	J	Q	U	S	A	M	O	H	T	K	C	A	J	C	X	P
N	L	A	V	T	H	D	R	D	T	S	B	Z	H	X	H	E	O
N	I	M	B	U	D	Y	M	K	N	Z	B	T	B	Y	U	Y	F
A	V	G	W	S	C	M	T	E	D	D	T	Z	Z	C	R	X	Z
B	I	O	N	Z	Q	A	H	G	Y	U	Q	F	Z	S	C	B	K
N	C	D	S	Y	C	R	J	J	Y	X	G	Q	F	K	H	J	I
I	V	Y	W	J	F	A	J	S	I	G	C	Y	E	D	L	A	E
M	H	J	Y	P	P	U	X	Z	B	L	H	X	L	N	Z	F	P
A	B	L	P	O	A	D	W	R	B	T	K	U	Y	T	V	M	D
J	W	R	F	V	D	E	T	Q	O	B	V	Q	I	K	U	C	K
N	R	K	V	D	W	R	Q	F	O	L	P	C	D	T	G	X	H
E	L	N	G	O	L	S	D	X	Q	X	C	C	J	Y	R	W	K
B	C	E	I	V	N	W	O	R	B	Q	E	I	L	L	A	H	H

Find These Words

AME-CHURCH WILBERFORCE BENJAMINBANNEKER
HALLIEQBROWN LADYMARAUDERS JACKTHOMAS
CIVILWAR MAROONANDGOLD

Directions: Read and answer the questions. These are your opinions so the answers will vary.

Would you rather ride a bike or a scooter?

What HBCU would you like to visit? Why?

Share a special memory you shared with family.

Directions: Unscramble the words below about CSU. See if you can get the bonus word.

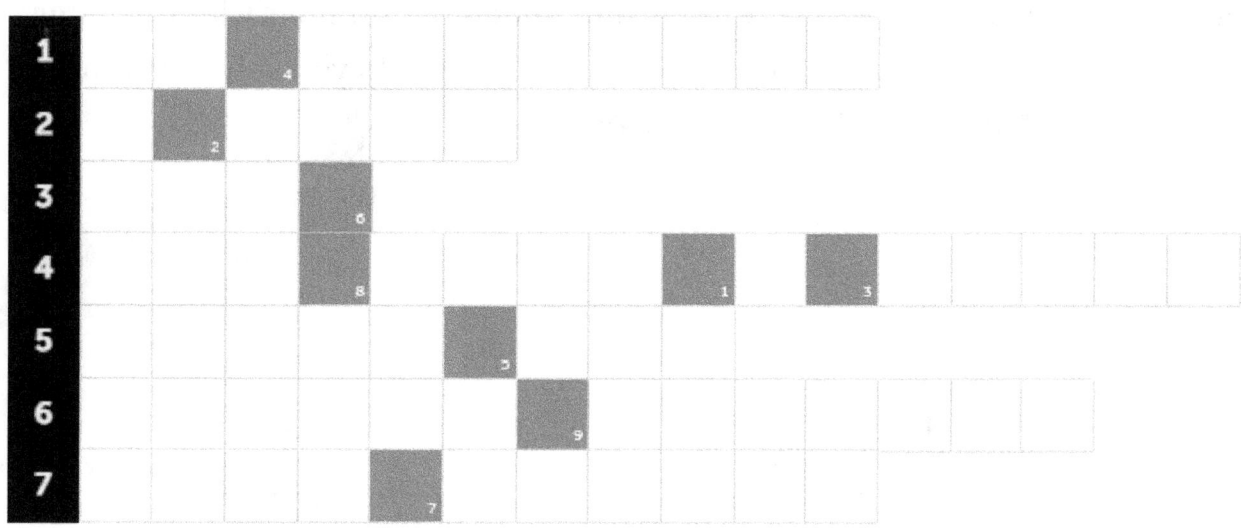

BONUS WORD

Unscramble Words
1) tcpsn-raaeg   **2)** anmoor   **3)** dlgo
4) ugmrshalotohlard   **5)** crchehaum   **6)** acrehswhyselle
7) rrwofebicel

Directions: This is the WGLT Challenge. Solve the cryptogram. As the puzzle solver, you need to find which number belongs to which character. And this can be pretty challenging! You will need to match the number with the letter. There are some letters given to you below. This will help you solve the other words and unlock more characters. **Good Luck.**

MARCH 2, 1867 – PRESENT

LEFT BLANK ON PURPOSE

Howard University

Howard University

Howard University

Howard University

Howard University

Howard University

Directions: read the bio below and answer the following questions.

Howard University (HU) is a private federally chartered HBCU. HU was founded in 1867 in Washington, D.C., and was named after General Oliver Otis Howard, who was a Civil War hero. The university offers undergraduate, graduate and professional degrees in more than 120 programs, which is more than any other (HBCU) in the nation. The historic main campus sits on a hilltop in Northwest Washington a few blocks away from the storied U Street and Howard Theatre. HU is two miles from the U.S. Capitol. The university's motto is "Veritas et Utilitas," which means "Truth and Service." This motto represents a key part of HU's identity. HU established the first Black law school in the nation. Five of the Divine Nine fraternities and sororities were founded at HU: Alpha Kappa Alpha sorority (1908), Delta Sigma Theta sorority (1913), Zeta Phi Beta sorority (1920), Omega Psi Phi fraternity (1911) and Phi Beta Sigma fraternity (1914). HU produces more on-campus African American Ph.D.s than any other university in the world.

1. What city was Howard founded in?
    A. Washington D.C.
    B. Atlanta, GA
    C. New York City, NY
2. Which sorority didn't get founded at Howard?
    A. Alpha Kappa Alpha
    B. Zeta Phi Beta
    C. Sigma Gamma Rho
3. What was HU first at doing at the University?
    A. first black medical school
    B. first black law school
    C. first black IT school

Directions: Answer the questions, to solve the crossword puzzle. You can use the internet if you get stuck on any question.

Across

2) Howard University offers four selective _____ for its most high-achieving undergraduate students.

5) Howard University campus, often referred to as "_____", is in northwest Washington, D. C.

6) _____ was the first sitting president to speak at Howard University.

Down

1) Howard hall was renovated and made a _____ for women.

3) Howard University has a _____ run commercial radio station WHUR-FM 96.3, also known as Howard University Radio.

4) Howard University was named after _____ Oliver O. Howard, a Civil War hero.

23

Directions: Read and answer the questions. These are your opinions so the answers will vary.

Would you rather stay up late or go to bed early?

What's your favorite fraternity or sorority? Why?

Where do you hope to live someday?

Directions: Unscramble the words below about HU. See if you can get the bonus word.

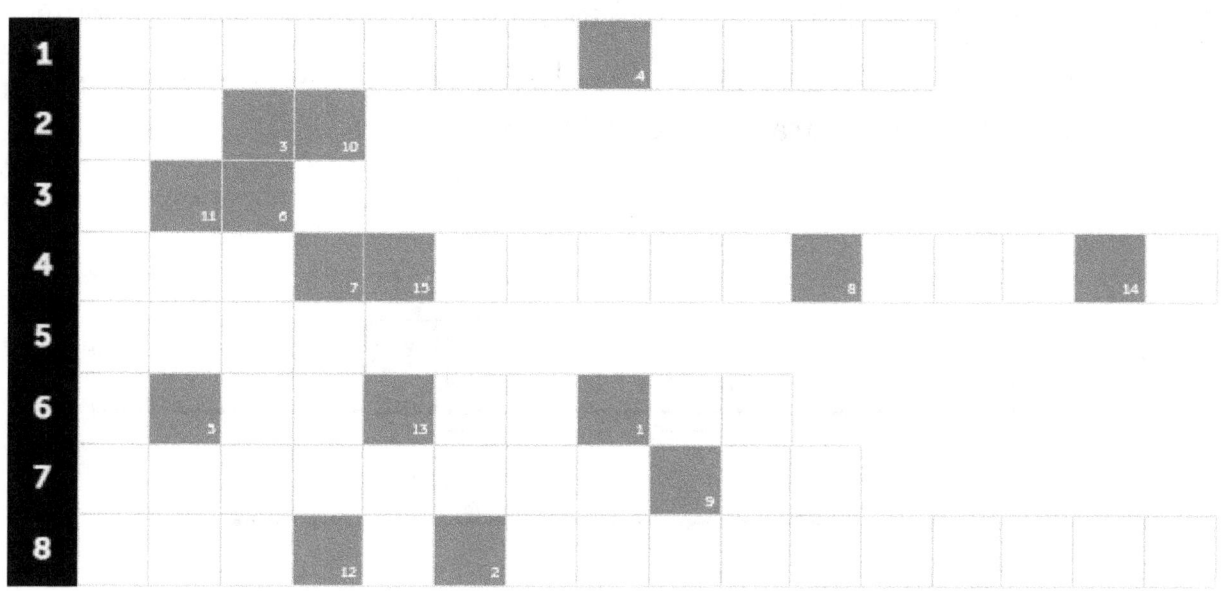

BONUS WORD

Unscramble Words

1) acosinwdgnht
2) uelb
3) ygra
4) faryrndweciikeea
5) eblu
6) llhtepitho
7) snoriwodhab
8) wlioovdisahertro

Directions: This is the WGLT Challenge. Solve the cryptogram. As the puzzle solver, you need to find which number belongs to which character. And this can be pretty challenging! You will need to match the number with the letter. There are some letters given to you below. This will help you solve the other words and unlock more characters. **Good Luck.**

Alcorn State
University

Alcorn State
University

1871 – PRESENT

LEFT BLANK ON PURPOSE

Alcorn State

University

Alcorn State

University

Directions: read the bio below and answer the following questions.

Alcorn University became Alcorn Agricultural and Mechanical College and then Alcorn State University (ASU). It is a public historically Black land-grant university that emphasizes intellectual development and lifelong learning through the integration of diverse pedagogies, applied and basic research, cultural and professional programs and public service and outreach programs. It also provides access to globally competitive academic and research programs. ASU was founded in 1871 in Lorman, MS, on the site of Oakland College, which had become defunct due to the start of the Civil War. ASU was the first Black land-grant college in the US. It was named in honor of the sitting governor of Mississippi, James L. Alcorn. At first, the school exclusively enrolled Black men, but women were admitted in 1895. ASU is accredited and features seven schools and degree programs that cover more than 50 areas, including a nursing program and a Master of Business Administration program.

1. Where was ASU founded at?
    A. Jackson, MS
    B. Lorman, MS
    C. The Bill Cosby show
2. What was Alcorn University the first in the U.S. for?
    A. First HBCU
    B. First land grant college
    C. First all male college
3. What was on the ASU land before we were founded?
    A. A farm
    B. A jail house
    C. A college

Directions: Find the words associated with Alcorn State University.

D	S	C	C	A	Q	M	Q	E	M	M	I	M	X	N	R	N
X	O	F	M	Q	L	B	O	A	M	G	P	N	V	N	W	M	U
C	U	L	E	I	E	V	F	A	X	H	N	D	D	P	S	Z	T
Z	N	N	T	L	S	T	J	C	N	F	A	T	A	F	I	N	A
C	D	H	K	U	E	S	S	T	N	A	R	G	E	C	A	P	S
R	S	X	W	G	B	C	I	S	P	S	G	O	W	G	P	A	J
P	O	Q	L	O	S	H	I	S	A	N	J	R	H	Q	T	M	E
S	F	A	E	L	U	A	X	A	S	S	E	V	A	R	B	F	H
I	D	C	S	D	X	W	C	Y	N	I	S	V	I	E	M	H	X
N	Y	X	I	E	O	Q	S	Z	Z	A	P	I	Y	I	S	G	U
S	N	M	B	N	Y	F	K	L	A	Q	V	P	S	E	R	X	T
Q	-	X	T	G	P	T	G	S	P	R	U	E	I	P	I	V	S
A	O	S	F	I	L	X	W	L	T	F	F	A	W	K	K	T	O
G	-	I	B	R	K	C	O	L	L	E	G	E	F	U	N	D	A
I	M	E	Z	L	J	V	W	I	P	O	X	H	H	N	W	N	A
I	I	A	D	S	S	X	I	E	L	C	U	F	H	G	H	U	O
W	T	S	L	E	V	E	R	M	A	R	I	H	L	J	D	W	F
J	E	X	X	C	B	G	A	L	H	U	Y	D	Q	S	W	V	D

Find These Words

COLLEGEFUND   BRAVES   HIRAMREVELS
MISSISSIPPI   SOUNDSOFDYN-O-MITE   GOLDENGIRLS
FELECIANAVE   SPACEGRANTS

Directions: Read and answer the questions. These are your opinions so the answers will vary.

Would you rather play video games or play outside?

What's your favorite vegetable or fruit?

Describe the most beautiful place you've ever been.

Directions: Unscramble the words below about ASU. See if you can get the bonus word.

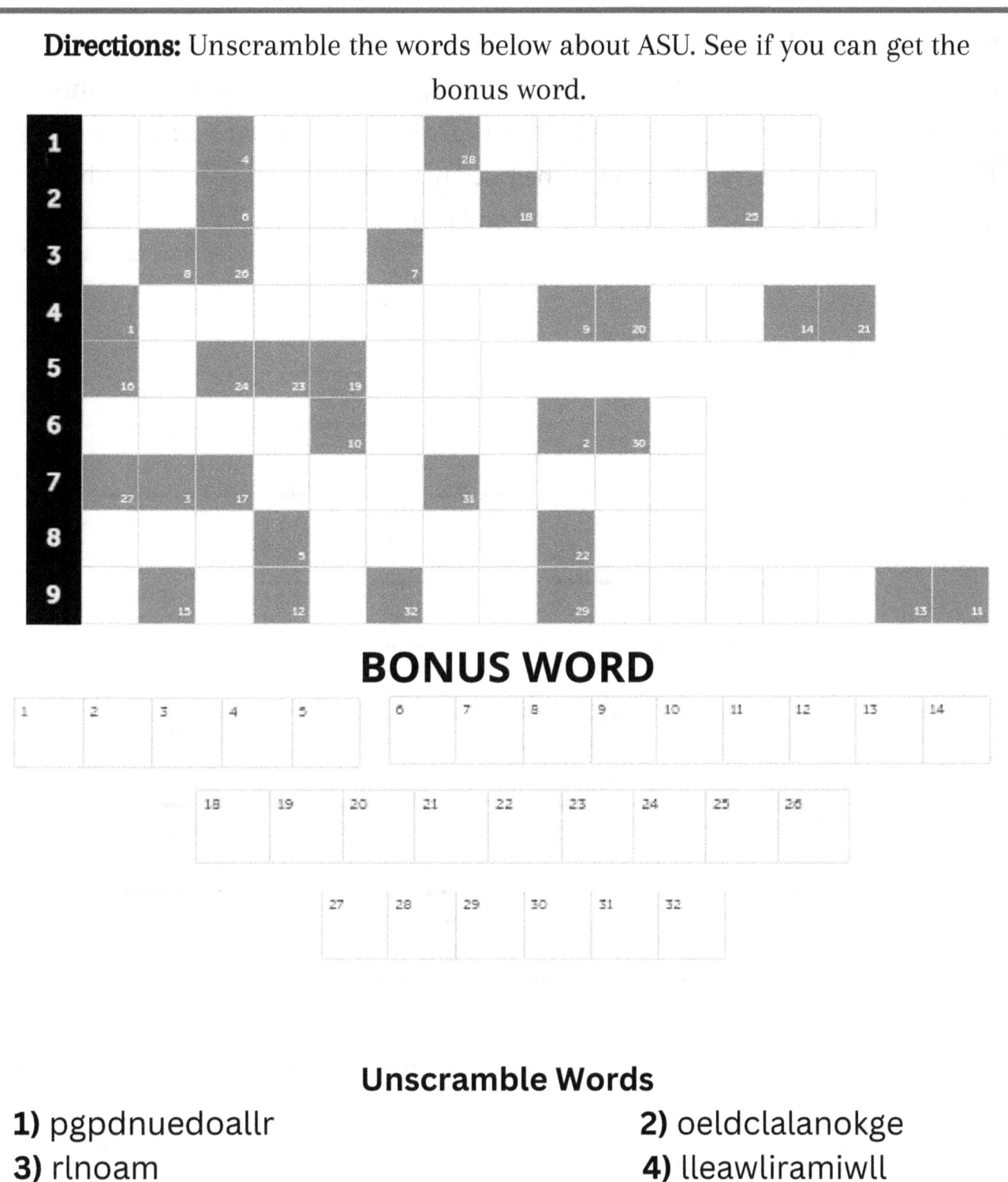

BONUS WORD

Unscramble Words

1) pgpdnuedoallr
2) oeldclalanokge
3) rlnoam
4) lleawliramiwll
5) tnacehz
6) slitvichgir
7) greravsedme
8) avalieeecnf
9) rnoeggecdatlnall

Directions: This is the WGLT Challenge. Solve the cryptogram. As the puzzle solver, you need to find which number belongs to which character. And this can be pretty challenging! You will need to match the number with the letter. There are some letters given to you below. This will help you solve the other words and unlock more characters. **Good Luck.**

Xavier University of
Louisiana

Xavier University of
Louisiana

OCTOBER 6, 1925 – PRESENT

LEFT BLANK ON PURPOSE

Xavier University of Louisiana

Xavier University of Louisiana

Directions: read the bio below and answer the following questions.

Xavier University Preparatory School, which is now called Xavier University of Louisiana (XULA), is a private HBCU and is the only Catholic HBCU. XULA tries to contribute to the promotion of a more just and humane society by preparing its students to assume roles of leadership and service in a global society. XULA was founded on October 6, 1925, in Louisiana, MO, by Katharine Drexel in an effort to help educate and evangelize Native Americans and African Americans. Katharine named the school after her father, Francis Xavier. She was trying to fill the void of Catholic education for young Black people in the South during Jim Crow. In 1925, XULA established the College of Liberal Arts and Sciences. In 1927, a College of Pharmacy was opened. XULA was the first Catholic university that was founded by a saint. Katharine Drexel was canonized as a saint by Pope John Paul II.

1. What was the universities name at the start?
   A. Xavier University
   B. Xavier University Preparatory School
   C. Xavier University of Louisiana
2. What year did XULA establish a pharmacy school?
   A. 1927
   B. 1925
   C. 1915
3. XULA is the only ____ HBCU?
   A. All Woman
   B. All Male
   C. Catholic

Directions: Answer the questions, to solve the crossword puzzle. You can use the internet if you get stuck on any question.

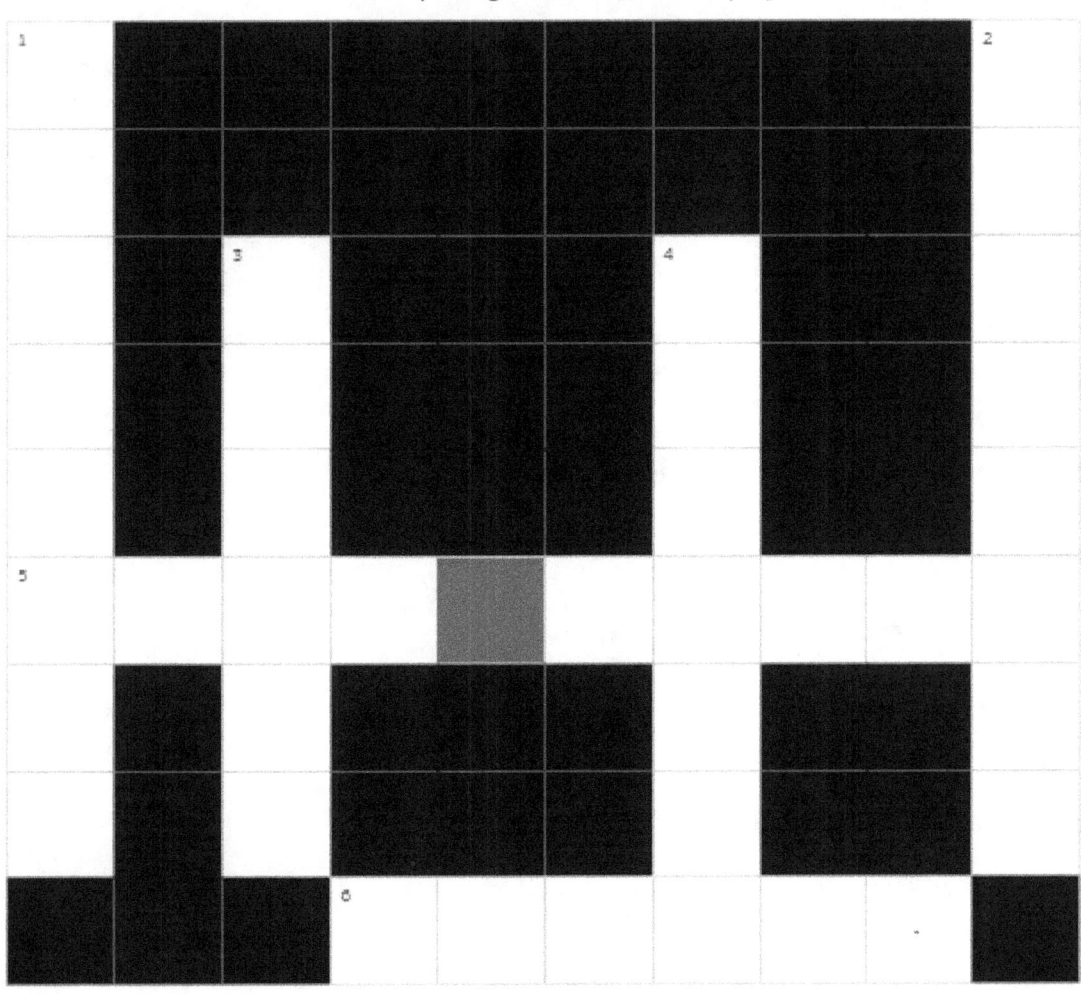

Across

5) Xavier of Louisiana mascot is a _____.

6) Xavier of Louisiana ranks third in National Institutes of _____.

Down

1) Xavier of Louisiana was recognized as the number three HBCU by U.S. News "Best _____" Guide 2021.

2) Xavier of Louisiana was designated as a _____ Friendly School.

3) Xavier of Louisiana is a nationally recognized leader in the STEM and _____ sciences fields.

4) Xavier of Louisiana is number one in the nation for producing the most African American graduates who successfully complete _____ school as of 2022.

Directions: Read and answer the questions. These are your opinions so the answers will vary.

Would you rather get up early or sleep late?

What's your favorite activity to do at recess?

Share a special memory you had with a friend.

Directions: Unscramble the words below about XULA. See if you can get the bonus word.

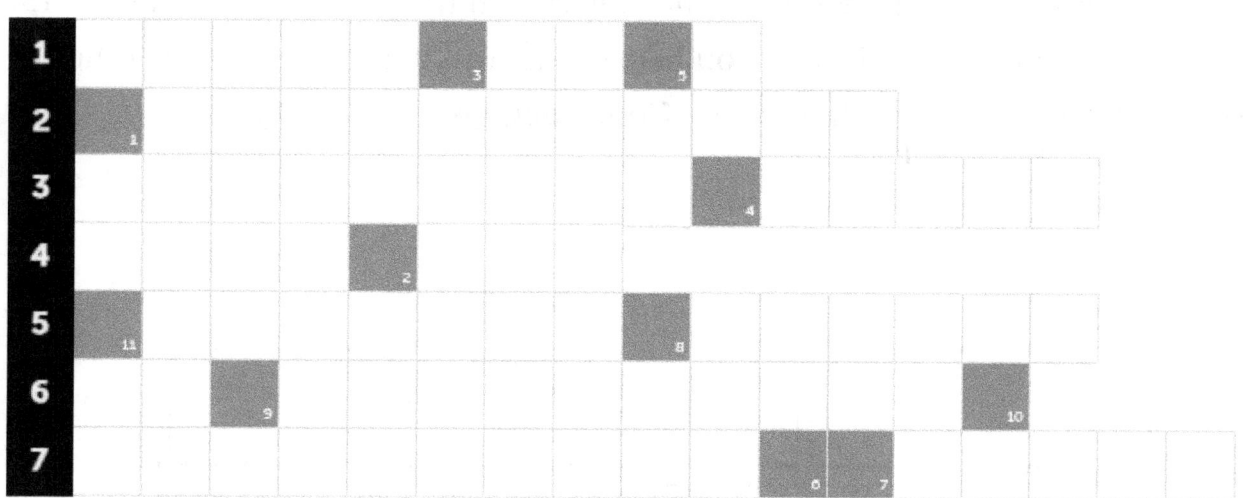

BONUS WORD

| 1 | 2 | 3 | 4 | | 5 | 6 | 7 | 8 | 9 | 10 | 11 |

Unscramble Words

1) nrnlaewose 2) wdtoaehnldgi 3) kxtirleaerdhane
4) ialhotcc 5) arirplsngeoereu 6) nylvrreecrtedo
7) cldtehdnyraaugroi

Directions: This is the WGLT Challenge. Solve the cryptogram. As the puzzle solver, you need to find which number belongs to which character. And this can be pretty challenging! You will need to match the number with the letter. There are some letters given to you below. This will help you solve the other words and unlock more characters. **Good Luck.**

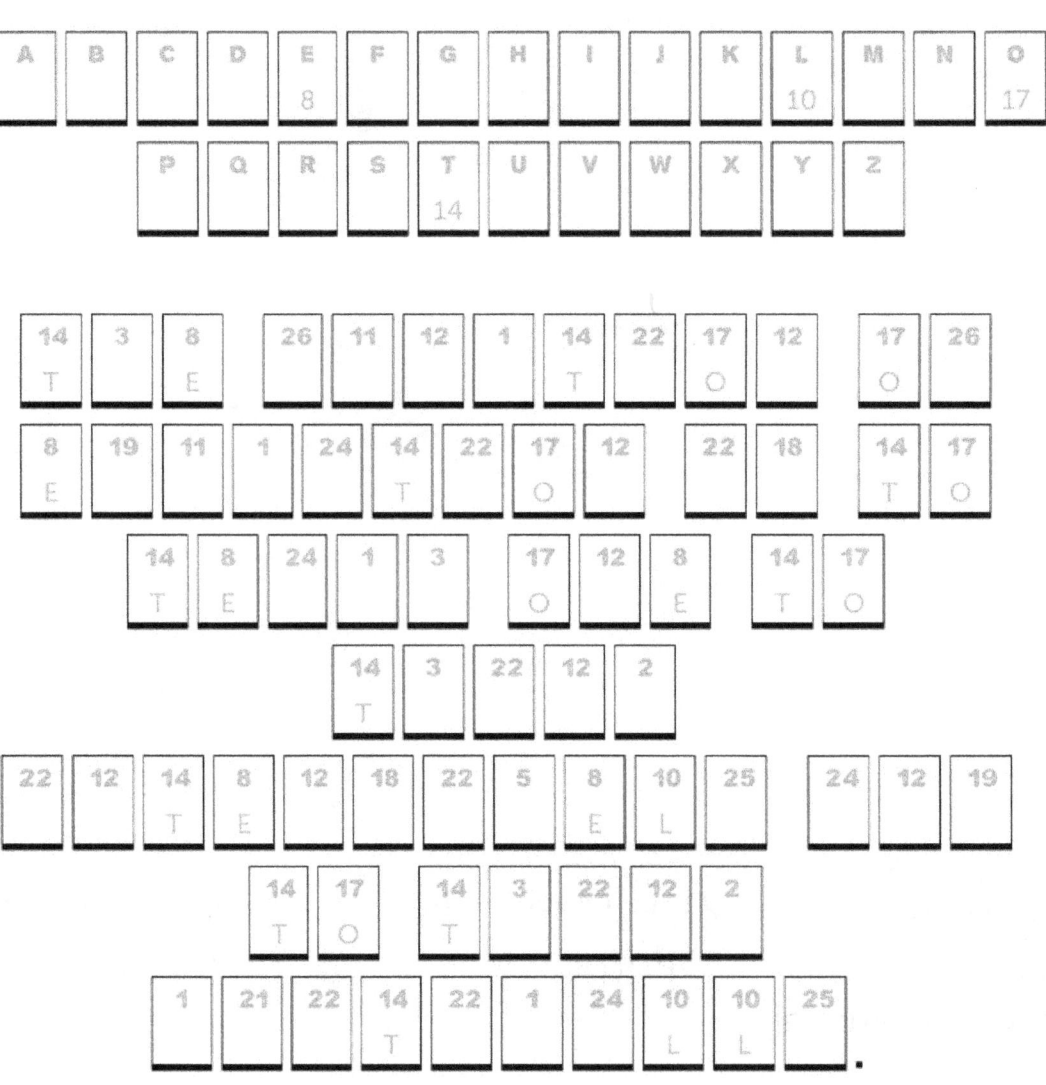

Elizabeth City State
University

Elizabeth City State
University

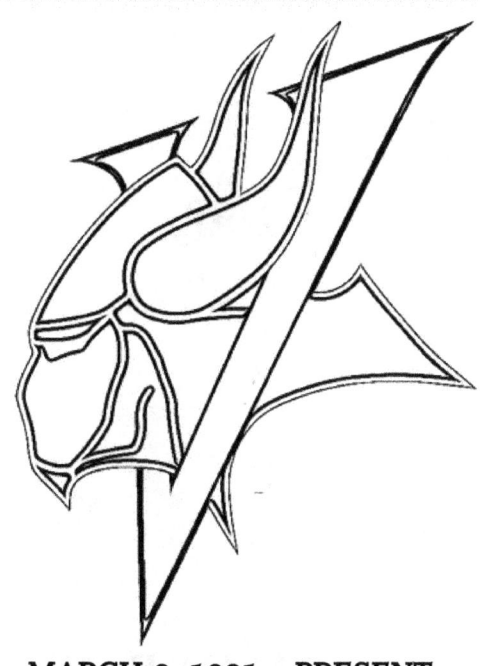

MARCH 3, 1891 – PRESENT

LEFT BLANK ON PURPOSE

Elizabeth City State

University

Elizabeth City State

University

Directions: read the bio below and answer the following questions.

Elizabeth City State Colored Normal School, which is now called Elizabeth City State University (ECSU), is a public HBCU that promotes economic, social and environmental progress for the people of northeastern North Carolina and the entire nation. ECSU was founded on March 3, 1891, in Elizabeth City, NC, by the North Carolina General Assembly. Hugh Cale sponsored House Bill 383, which established a normal (teaching) school for "teaching and training teachers of the colored race to teach in the common schools of North Carolina." ECSU started as a two-year normal school, but in 1937, it was elevated to a four-year teachers' college. In 1939, the name was officially changed to Elizabeth City State Teachers College. In 1963, the N.C. General Assembly changed the institution's name from Elizabeth City State Teachers College to Elizabeth City State College. In 1969, the college became Elizabeth City State University.

1. What was the colleges name in the beginning?
    A. Elizabeth City State College
    B. Elizabeth City State Colored Normal School
    C. Elizabeth City State University
2. What year did the college become an university?
    A. 1963
    B. 1939
    C. 1969
3. What was ECSU before becoming a 4 year college?
    A. It's always been a 4 year college
    B. It was a 2 year college
    C. It was a teaching school

Directions: Find the words associated with Elizabeth City State University.

```
D H U M A N S T U D I E S O T L N E
I Y S L S O C M Y E P S T Z O B U Y
G B E X S D L M O A E D C Q O L H N
I A G X G O X U D W C A S H Z U A W
T X B J N L N R F U N H W V E E G R
A V Q Z I V S Z E P E X N T A A N V
L K X K K H E A L Z I M U R X N V S
M M Q W I Q Q P A L C C U P H D R -
E V G Q V F W D G U S Q O L J W Z F
D I E W J S T C E E Y C I C E H V M
I N A D Y N C B K M R M K L X I Y N
A E O S X Q K D I S A U Z K I T J K
W I H B M W F J M Y T O V T H E W I
I C A L W G A H Q Z I L J L J Z D R
B M S E C N E I C S L A R U T A N B
N N Y F E A T G T F I O W C X S P X
B M V O Z T M R K D M U Q D X D L Y
W P S D R A I L L I H Y N O H T N A
```

Find These Words

DIGITALMEDIA
HUMANSTUDIES
WRVS-FM
MIKEGALE
BLUEANDWHITE

NATURALSCIENCES
MILITARYSCIENCE
VIKINGS
ANTHONYHILLIARD

Directions: Read and answer the questions. These are your opinions so the answers will vary.

Would you rather ride a bike or a scooter?

What's your favorite book & why?

What are you most excited about doing when you are a teen then college student and then an adult?

Directions: Unscramble the words below about ECSU. See if you can get the bonus word.

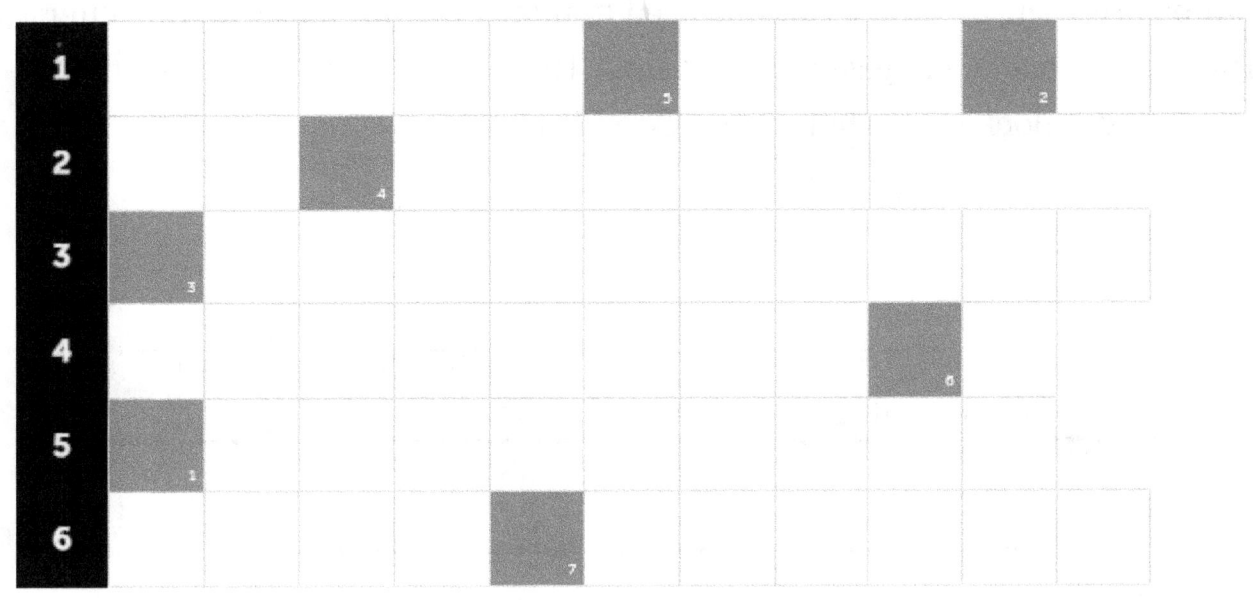

BONUS WORD

Unscramble Words

1) eaduweilnhbt
2) avintoai
3) xiiadrnkeor
4) hgrphejtou
5) aatvusslri
6) vioitidsnow

49

Directions: This is the WGLT Challenge. Solve the cryptogram. As the puzzle solver, you need to find which number belongs to which character. And this can be pretty challenging! You will need to match the number with the letter. There are some letters given to you below. This will help you solve the other words and unlock more characters. **Good Luck.**

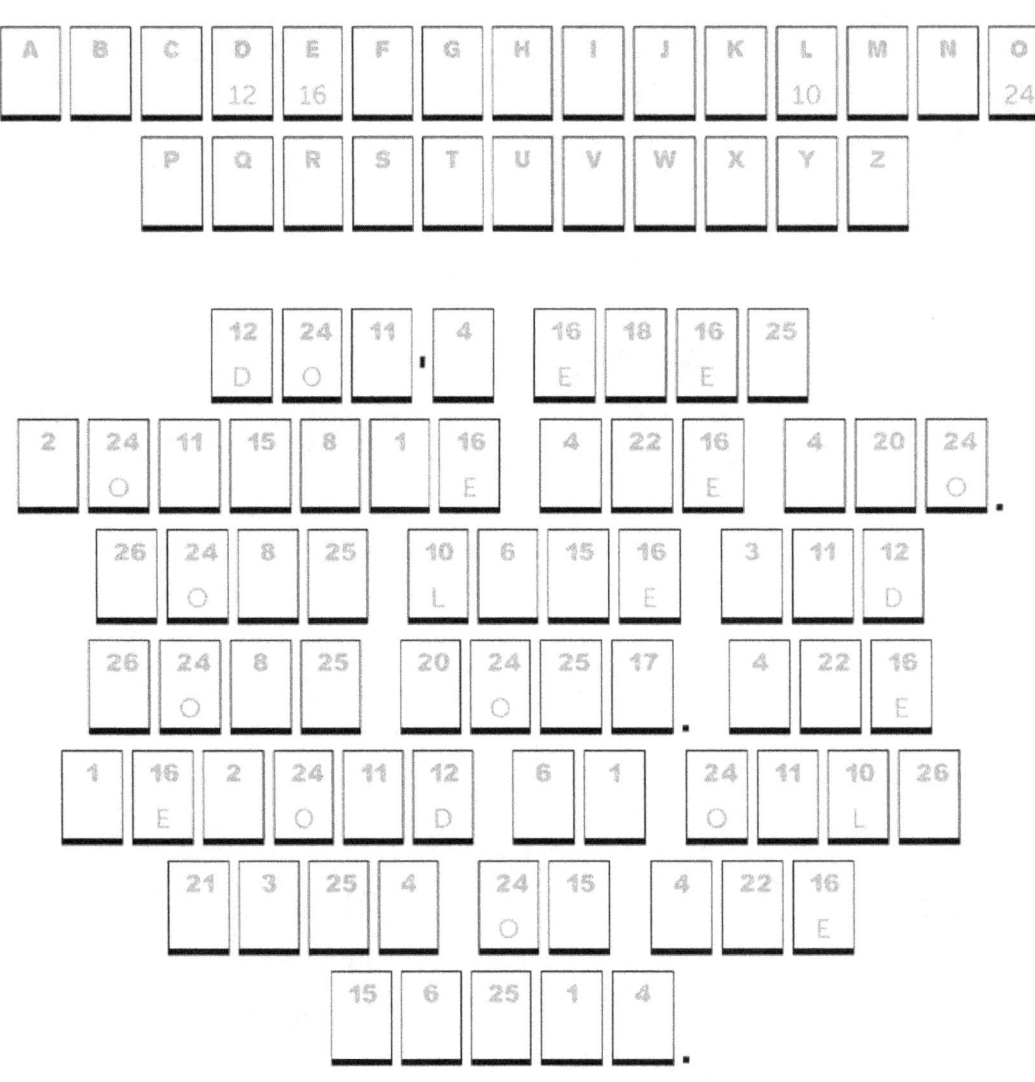

APRIL 1, 1868 –PRESENT

LEFT BLANK ON PURPOSE

Hampton University

Hampton University

Hampton University

Hampton University

Hampton University

Hampton University

Directions: read the bio below and answer the following questions.

Hampton Agricultural and Industrial School, which is now called Hampton University (HIU), is a private HBCU that is dedicated to promoting learning, building character and preparing promising students for positions of leadership and service. HIU was founded on April 1, 1868, in Hampton, VA, which is where Mary Smith Peake used to gather her pupils under a large oak. In 1863, the Emancipation Proclamation was read here – the first place in the Confederate states. From then on, the large tree was called the Emancipation Oak and became a National Historic Landmark and a symbol of the promise of education for all, even in the face of adversity. The new school was established on the grounds of a former plantation named "Little Scotland," which had a view of Hampton Roads. HIU houses the Hampton University Museum which is the nation's oldest African American museum and one of the oldest museums in Virginia. The museum was established in 1868. HIU was legally chartered in 1870 as a land-grant school.

1. What national landmark is on HIU campus?
   A. Booker T. Washington National Monument
   B. Emancipation Oak
   C. The Mere Distinction of Colour
2. What year was HIU founded?
   A. 1863
   B. 1868
   C. 1870
3. What can you only find on HIU?
   A. Hampton University Museum
   B. Maggie Walker National Historic Site
   C. Black Soldiers Memorial

Directions: Answer the questions, to solve the crossword puzzle. You can use the internet if you get stuck on any question.

Across

1) Hampton University consistently ranks among the _____ HBCUs in the nation.

3) Hampton University is the first and only HBCU to have 100% control of a _____.

5) Hampton University traces its roots to _____, who began in 1861 with outdoor classes for freedmen.

6) Hampton University established a formal education program for _____ to accommodate men who had been held as prisoners of war in 1878.

Down

2) Hampton University was established on the grounds of a former _____ named "Little Scotland."

4) Hampton University Museum was founded in 1868 and is the nation's _____ African-American museum.

Directions: Read and answer the questions. These are your opinions so the answers will vary.

Would you rather be a wizard or a superhero?

What's your favorite ice cream flavor?

Share a time when someone was extra kind to you.

Directions: Unscramble the words below about HIU. See if you can get the bonus word.

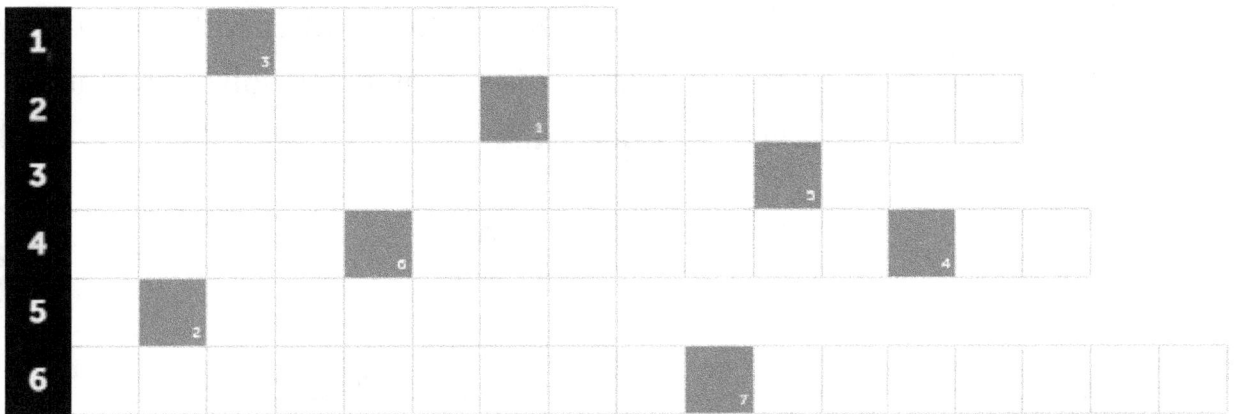

BONUS WORD

Unscramble Words

1) vgiiinar **2)** inrganmrotpyes **3)** lweenhitbadu
4) wimilaaldrlrlse **5)** ilciarwv **6)** oowtsabtnignhreko

Directions: This is the WGLT Challenge. Solve the cryptogram. As the puzzle solver, you need to find which number belongs to which character. And this can be pretty challenging! You will need to match the number with the letter. There are some letters given to you below. This will help you solve the other words and unlock more characters. **Good Luck.**

Alabama State
University

Alabama State
University

1867 – PRESENT

LEFT BLANK ON PURPOSE

Alabama State University

Alabama State University

Directions: read the bio below and answer the following questions.

Lincoln Normal School of Marion, which is now known as Alabama State University (ASU), is a public HBCU that is committed to excellence in teaching, research and service. ASU provides a nurturing, holistic learning environment that is focused on teaching students to be global change agents and using philanthropy to create dynamic relationships that positively impact communities. ASU was founded on November 13, 1867, in Marion, AL. In 1887, the university moved to its new location in Montgomery, AL. The Alabama State Supreme Court ruling forced the school to change its name to the Normal School for Colored Students. In 1928, the school became a four-year institution and in 1929, it became State Teachers College. In 1948, the school changed its name to Alabama State College for Negroes and then Alabama State College in 1954. In 1969, the State Board of Education, which was the governing body of the university at that time, approved another name change; the institution became Alabama State University.

1. Where was ASU located when it was founded?
   A. Montgomery, AL
   B. Mobile, AL
   C. Marion, AL
2. What year did I ASU move to Montgomery?
   A. 1867
   B. 1887
   C. 1928
3. What name did the University start out with?
   A. Lincoln Normal School of Marion
   B. Alabama State University
   C. Alabama State College

Directions: Find the words associated with ASU.

E	G	A	K	H	L	U	P	K	C	F	E	F	Z	F	Z	D	X
A	V	Z	N	V	N	P	Y	R	E	M	O	G	T	N	O	M	A
A	E	O	W	I	R	F	H	Z	Y	Y	Y	M	B	G	U	T	M
M	K	R	T	N	A	V	R	T	B	A	V	B	Q	I	A	G	R
G	Y	N	O	O	T	M	E	Q	W	D	F	A	L	N	D	P	J
W	G	F	K	S	O	S	Z	C	Y	L	I	N	M	A	F	S	X
S	P	E	S	X	P	E	U	C	F	O	R	B	G	A	C	Y	P
T	G	M	O	B	H	A	X	H	T	G	D	E	D	D	K	K	A
R	A	M	A	R	D	N	C	P	P	D	Y	L	C	L	G	P	N
A	X	Z	F	V	G	R	H	E	M	L	D	M	B	I	Q	G	C
L	U	E	X	D	V	E	I	A	S	O	J	E	G	R	X	S	H
A	T	D	E	W	T	B	C	K	M	T	A	G	S	T	U	V	H
R	X	R	A	V	U	S	D	A	B	A	U	B	V	O	H	S	W
E	U	D	E	R	W	Z	M	J	R	J	B	D	F	O	I	Y	G
B	L	W	C	C	Z	G	Z	C	A	D	I	A	I	C	R	O	Q
I	N	M	S	T	E	N	R	O	H	Y	D	A	L	E	E	J	J
L	F	J	A	K	U	K	A	C	B	M	P	E	K	A	S	Y	G
L	Q	Z	B	D	N	U	F	E	G	E	L	L	O	C	O	U	Y

Find These Words

OLDGOLD	ALABAMA	GEORGECARD
AEROSPACESTUDIES	LIBERALARTS	BLACK
LADYHORNETS	COLLEGEFUND	MONTGOMERY

Directions: Read and answer the questions. These are your opinions so the answers will vary.

Would you rather work in a group or work alone?

What's your favorite hobby or after school activity?

Where do you want to go to college?

Directions: Unscramble the words below about ASU. See if you can get the bonus word.

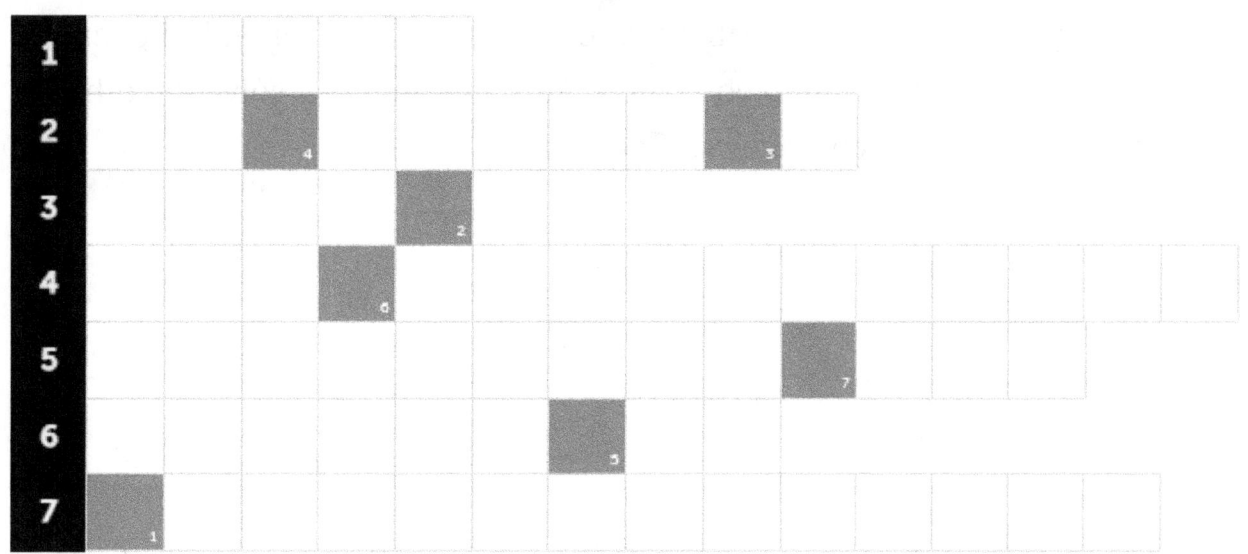

BONUS WORD

1	2	3	4	5	6	7

Unscramble Words

1) blakc   **2)** mronmgotye   **3)** oogldld
4) oafbtawrodcnran   **5)** nourqrisojtns   **6)** abekcbtll
7) hchenlssteceai

Directions: This is the WGLT Challenge. Solve the cryptogram. As the puzzle solver, you need to find which number belongs to which character. And this can be pretty challenging! You will need to match the number with the letter. There are some letters given to you below. This will help you solve the other words and unlock more characters. **Good Luck.**

Solution:

25	9	1	19		1	19	25	9	15
T	H	I	S		I	S	T	H	E

10	15	7	1	11		11	1	11	7	18	3
B	E	G	I	N		N	I	N	G	O	F

8	11	14	25	9	1	11	7		14	18	24
A	N	Y	T	H	I	N	G		Y	O	U

20	8	11	25		25	18	2	18
W	A	N	T		T	O	D	O.

"THIS IS THE BEGINNING OF ANYTHING YOU WANT TO DO."

FEB. 14, 1867 – PRESENT

Morehouse College

Morehouse College

Morehouse College

Morehouse College

Morehouse College

Morehouse College

Directions: read the bio below and answer the following questions.

Augusta Institute, which is now called Morehouse College, is a private men's **HBCU** that is dedicated to developing men with disciplined minds who will lead lives of leadership and service. It was founded on February 14, 1867, in Augusta, GA, in the basement of Springfield Baptist Church by Rev. William Jefferson White, Rev. Richard C. Coulter and Rev. Edmund Turney just a couple of years after the American Civil War. In 1879, the institution moved from Augusta to Atlanta and changed its name to Atlanta Baptist Seminary. In 1897, the school changes its name again to Atlanta Baptist College. In 1913, the college was renamed Morehouse College in honor of Henry L. Morehouse. The institution was originally founded to educate African American men in theology and education. Morehouse College is one of three all-male private colleges in the US. The other two are Wabash College and Hampden-Sydney College.

1. Where was the college location when it was founded?
    A. Atlanta, GA
    B. Savannah, GA
    C. Augusta, GA
2. What year did we adopt the name Morehouse?
    A. 1897
    B. 1913
    C. 1887
3. Which is not a private all male college?
    A. Spelman College
    B. Wabash College
    C. Morehouse College

70

Directions: Answer the questions, to solve the crossword puzzle. You can use the internet if you get stuck on any question.

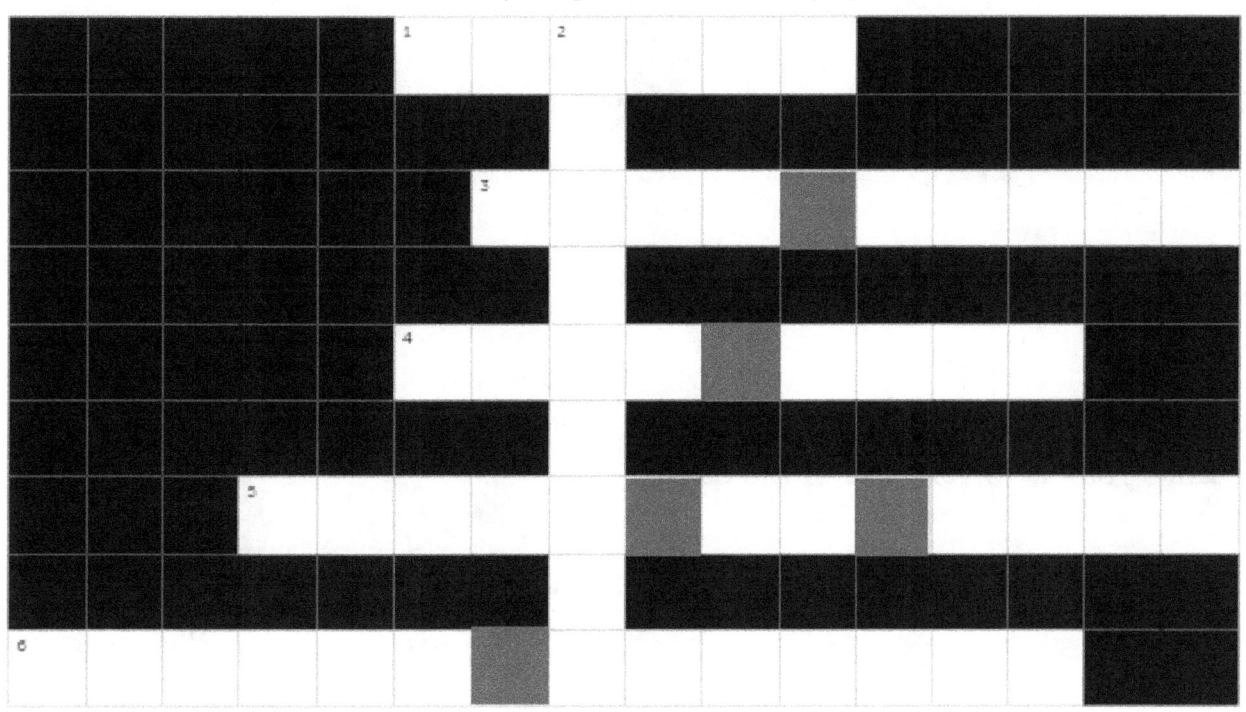

Across

1) Morehouse College colors are _____ and white.

3) Morehouse College is a member of the American _____ Association (AMTA).

4) Morehouse College _____ performed at Martin Luther King Jr.'s funeral.

5) Morehouse College Marching Band, better known as the _____ has performed at Super Bowl XXVIII.

6) Morehouse College offers over thirty majors and the _____ Honors Program.

Down

2) President Obama became the first sitting president in three-quarters of a century to deliver a commencement address, the first was President _____.

Directions: Read and answer the questions. These are your opinions so the answers will vary.

Would you rather play hide-and-seek or dodgeball?

What's your favorite meal of the day?

Share about a time you learned an important life lesson.

Directions: Unscramble the words below about Morehouse College. See if you can get the bonus word.

BONUS WORD

Unscramble Words

1) amrnieotrgo
2) dtaamohvdsi
3) etwih
4) ciilvarw
5) anrmoo
6) eblguce
7) mteaabteed

Directions: This is the WGLT Challenge. Solve the cryptogram. As the puzzle solver, you need to find which number belongs to which character. And this can be pretty challenging! You will need to match the number with the letter. There are some letters given to you below. This will help you solve the other words and unlock more characters. **Good Luck.**

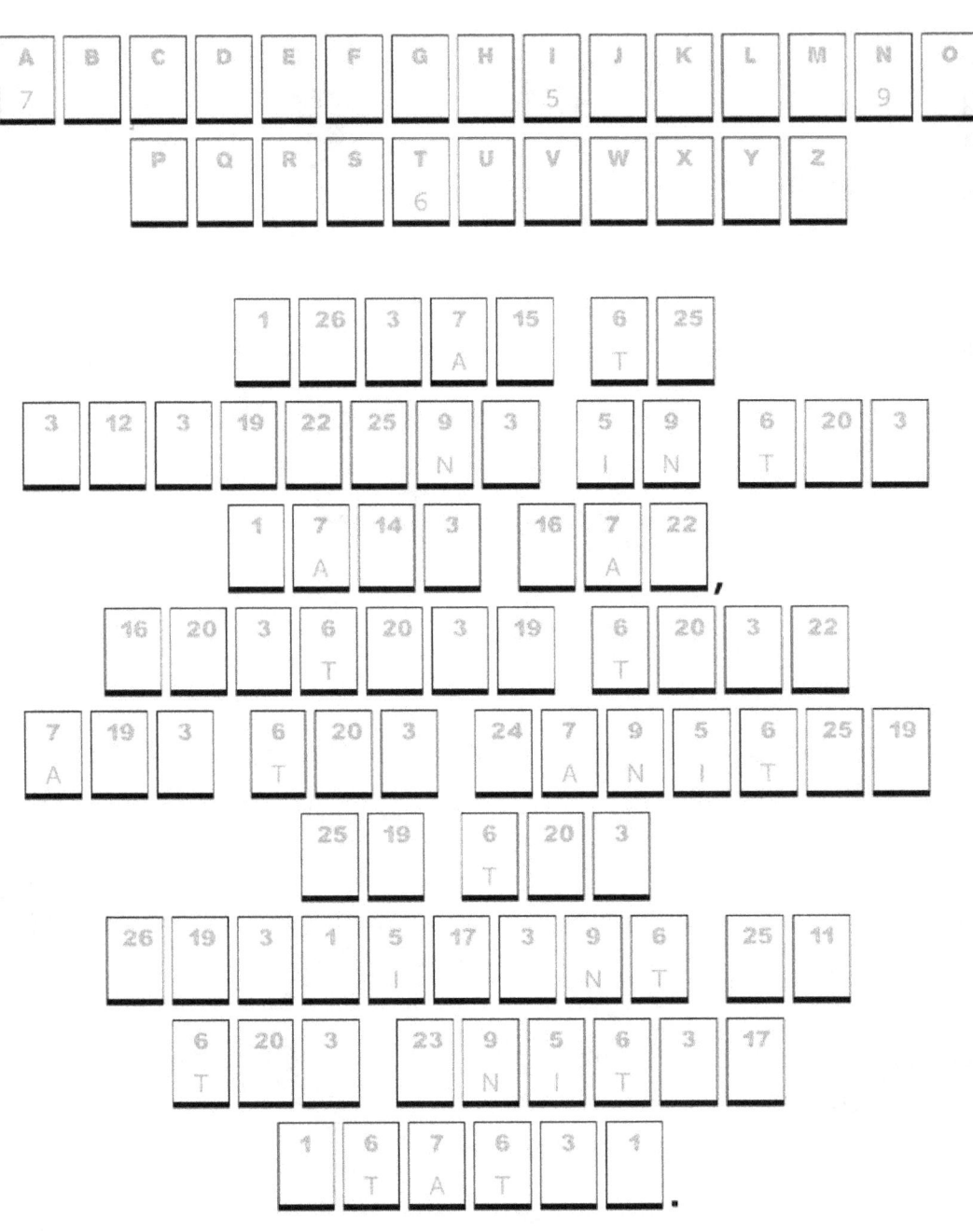

Southern University
and A&M College

Southern University
and A&M College

APRIL 10, 1880 – PRESENT

LEFT BLANK ON PURPOSE

Southern University
and A&M College

Southern University
and A&M College

Directions: read the bio below and answer the following questions.

Southern University for Colored Students, which is now known as Southern University and AGM College (Southern University, Southern, SUBR, or SU) is a public land-grant HBCU that is dedicated to a student-focused teaching and learning environment that creates global leadership opportunities for its diverse student population. It was founded on April 10, 1880, in Baton Rouge, LA. Over the years, the school has grown tremendously and is currently the largest HBCU in Louisiana. In 1974, a special session in the Louisiana Legislature established the Southern University System. The system consists of the following schools: Southern University and AGM College, Baton Rouge (SUBR; 1904); Southern University, New Orleans (SUNO; 1956); Southern University Law Center (SULC; 1947); Southern University Agricultural Center (SUAC; 2001); and Southern University, Shreveport (SUSLA; 1964). SUSLA is a two- year commuter college.

1. Which college isn't in the Southern University System?
   A. Southern University and A&M College
   B. Southern University
   C. Louisiana State University
2. What year was SUSLA established?
   A. 1904
   B. 1964
   C. 1956
3. There are __ college's in the Southern University System?
   A. 5
   B. 6
   C. 4

Directions: Find the words associated with Southern University.

```
R L G F X G O N A A B S W D Q B W T
H C A U R C Q P A S X W L D U T O Y
Q O A D C Y C S D X E L G H M N G T
R L S O Y V W R L M F P K N I Z O H
H L D B H J A V O W Y Z U R N Y L E
G E C U Q C A S J J U Z Q A T Y D H
Z G K S E B Y G Y X Q I H C D D Y U
C E E P C A J J U S A V U H I L M M
Y F N J F E J C U A I C D N R Q C A
J U V T X P S P V S R X U E X T L N
N N S J W Z P E R L G S E Y H Y N J
V D T K Q D Z E T A Q N L Z X L U
B Z W U E R U T L U C I R G A I Y K
R S K M E B I K K N A Q A Y K J W E
S J V X S L A C I N A H C E M B H B
Y G W E G W S P A C E A G E N T D O
D C X T S E G I D N R E H T U O S X
E I C O L U M B I A B L U E U T M P
```

Find These Words

AGRICULTURE   GOLD   LADYJAGUARS
SPACEAGENT   MECHANICAL   THEHUMANJUKEBOX
COLLEGEFUND   SOUTHERNDIGEST   COLUMBIABLUE

79

Directions: Read and answer the questions. These are your opinions so the answers will vary.

Would you rather have indoor or outdoor recess?

What's your favorite board or card game?

What do you think you might be doing in 10 years?

Directions: Unscramble the words below about SU. See if you can get the bonus word.

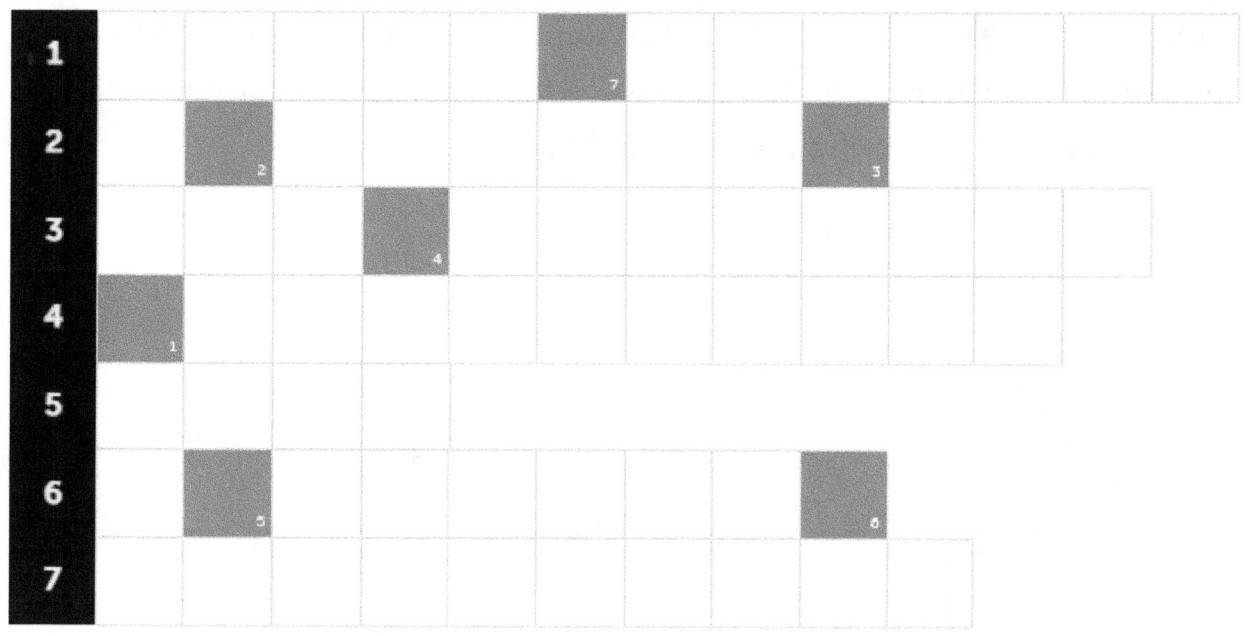

BONUS WORD

Unscramble Words

1) ihsslneisdedn   2) gonrebotau   3) umalelbbciou
4) hlaekjspocr   5) ogdl   6) lwntacere
7) hmiiteanus

Directions: This is the WGLT Challenge. Solve the cryptogram. As the puzzle solver, you need to find which number belongs to which character. And this can be pretty challenging! You will need to match the number with the letter. There are some letters given to you below. This will help you solve the other words and unlock more characters. **Good Luck.**

A	B	C	D	E	F	G	H	I	J	K	L	M	N	O
11				5		25								

P	Q	R	S	T	U	V	W	X	Y	Z
			20							

Row 1: 20(S) 7 11(A) 22 22   9 11(A) 23 22 1

Row 2: 23 7 18 24 10 13 5(E) 7 5(E) 16 2 20(S)

Row 3: 11(A) 24 5(E)   2 17 5(E)   8 5(E) 1   2 10

Row 4: 20(S) 2 11(A) 25(G) 25(G) 5(E) 24 23 16 25(G)   22 10 16 25(G)

Row 5: 2 5(E) 24 7   24 5(E) 20(S) 26 22 2 20(S) .

82

JULY 4, 1881 – PRESENT

LEFT BLANK ON PURPOSE

Tuskegee University

Tuskegee University

Tuskegee University

Tuskegee University

Tuskegee University

Tuskegee University

Directions: read the bio below and answer the following questions.

Tuskegee Normal School for Colored Teachers, which is now Tuskegee University (Tuskegee or TU), is a private land-grant HBCU that is dedicated to improving quality of life by impacting communities on the local, state, regional, national and international levels. It was founded on July 4, 1881, in Tuskegee, AL, in a one-room shanty near Butler Chapel AME Zion Church by George Campbell, a former slave owner and Lewis Adams, a tinsmith, former slave and community leader. Booker T. Washington was the first principal and intended to train students in skills, morals and religious life in addition to academic subjects. He urged the teachers whom he trained "to return to the plantation districts and show the people there how to put new energy and new ideas into farming as well as into the intellectual and moral and religious life of the people." In 1966, Tuskegee University became the first Black college to be designated as a Registered National Historic Landmark. In 1974, TU became the only Black college to be designated a National Historic Site.

1. Which abbreviation is not a Tuskegee University?
   A. TSU
   B. Tuskegee
   C. TU
2. What year did we become a historic landmark?
   A. 1974
   B. 1966
   C. 1968
3. We are the only HBCU that is what?
   A. A Catholic College
   B. All Women College
   C. National Historic Site

Directions: Answer the questions, to solve the crossword puzzle. You can use the internet if you get stuck on any question.

Across

1) Tuskegee University band is called The Marching _____ Band (MCP).

5) U.S. Army Air Corps established a _____ at Tuskegee Institute, using Moton Field.

6) Tuskegee University newspaper is called The TU _____.

Down

2) Tuskegee Institute collaborated with the United States government in the Tuskegee syphilis experiment by which the effects of deliberately untreated ___ were studied.

3) Tuskegee University was declared a National Historic _____ for the significance of its academic programs, its role in higher education for African-Americans and its status in United States history.

4) George Washington Carver was a ___ at Tuskegee University.

Directions: Read and answer the questions. These are your opinions so the answers will vary.

Would you rather go to a zoo or an aquarium?

What's your favorite snack to eat?

Describe the most amazing thing you've ever seen in real life.

Directions: Unscramble the words below about TU. See if you can get the bonus word.

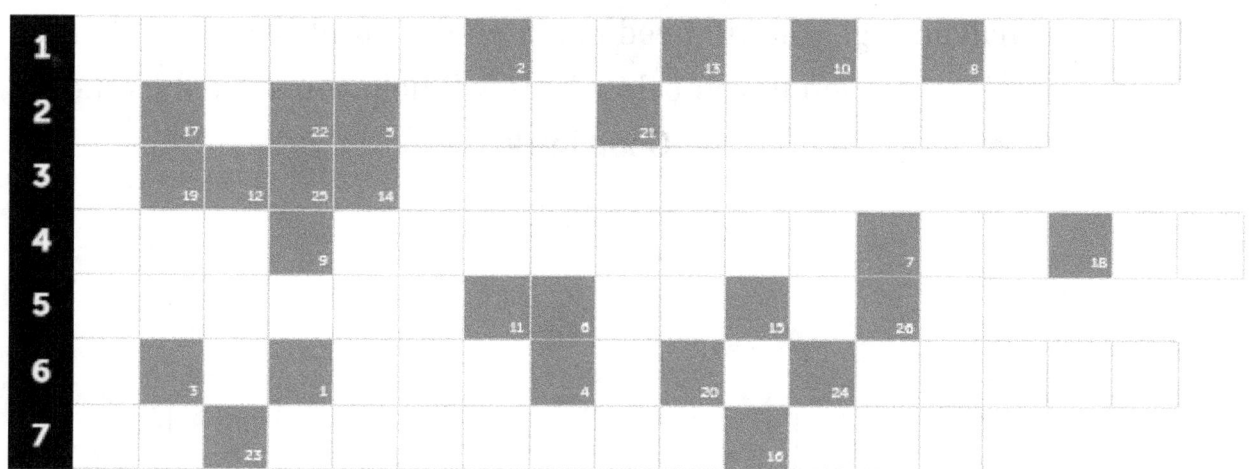

BONUS WORD

Unscramble Words

1) igonroaldclddsomn
2) rehroroistmcalt
3) rgtapsenca
4) ntaevireenciimdrye
5) kieensmugaeetr
6) obknhriegtstowona
7) wltoildinivads

Directions: This is the WGLT Challenge. Solve the cryptogram. As the puzzle solver, you need to find which number belongs to which character. And this can be pretty challenging! You will need to match the number with the letter. There are some letters given to you below. This will help you solve the other words and unlock more characters. **Good Luck.**

Solution:

Letter	A	B	C	D	E	F	G	H	I	J	K	L	M	N	O	P	Q	R	S	T	U	V	W	X	Y	Z
Number	22	–	25	11	10	–	7	23	8	–	19	24	–	14	5	26	–	3	16	9	20	–	15	–	4	21

Decoded message:

THE PEOPLE WHO
ARE CRAZY
ENOUGH TO THINK
THEY CAN CHANGE
THE WORLD ARE
THE ONES WHO DO.

Norfolk State University

Norfolk State University

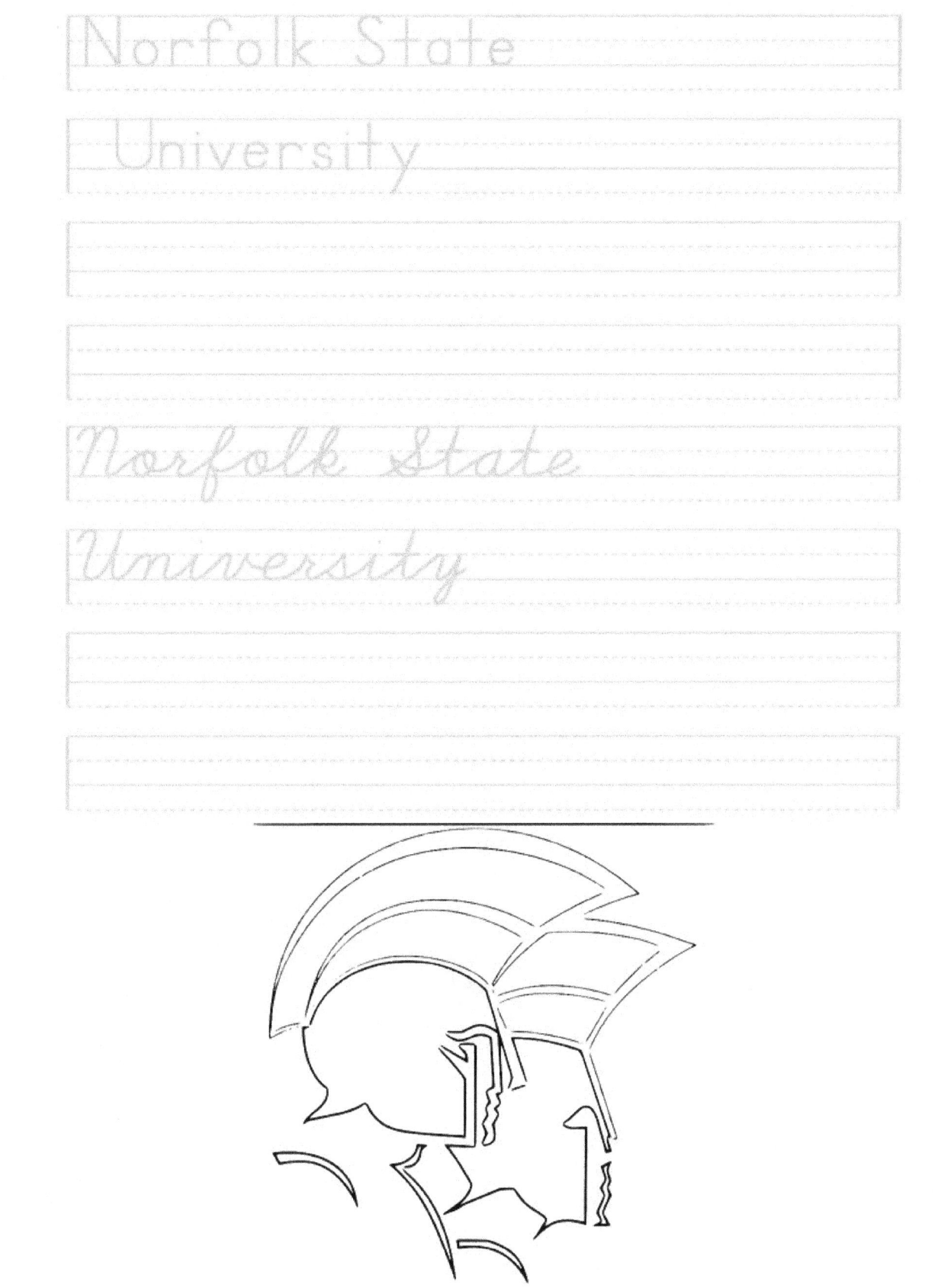

SEPTEMBER 18, 1935 – PRESENT

LEFT BLANK ON PURPOSE

Norfolk State

University

Norfolk State

University

Directions: read the bio below and answer the following questions.

Norfolk Unit of Virginia Union University, which is now called Norfolk State University (NSU), is a public HBCU that is dedicated to transforming students' lives through exemplary teaching, research and service. It was founded on September 18, 1935, in Norfolk, VA, in the midst of the Great Depression and began providing new and exciting possibilities for the region's youth.

Focusing on an arts and sciences curriculum with 13 subjects that included African American history, the Norfolk Unit of Virginia Union University began very modestly as a private Baptist institution. In 1942, the school became independent of VSU and was named Norfolk Polytechnic College. In 1944, as part of an act of the Virginia Legislature, the college became a part of Virginia State College (VSC). In 1969, the college separated from Virginia State College and was named Norfolk State College. In 1979, the General Assembly of Virginia changed the college's name to Norfolk State University.

1. What event was going on when the college was founded?
    A. The Boulder (Hoover) Dam is completed.
    B. World War II
    C. The Great Depression
2. What year did NSU split from VSC?
    A. 1944
    B. 1969
    C. 1979
3. What name did I NSU start with?
    A. Virginia State College
    B. Norfolk Unit of Virginia Union University
    C. Norfolk State College

Directions: Find the words associated with Norfolk State University.

```
T C K L O F R O N N T S E Y N Z W R
V I B K D Y T S T K H P R V H P S J
C K Q M I E B Y L S E A A T X Y J U
X Z X U H N H B Z K S R K I H T P X
Q C H C O G G J P X P T W Y C Y A Q
D W A I N I G R I V A A D P C X R Y
I P N O O N T E X V R N N U N Q E Z
V C P Q R E E Z Y X T L R E D V G E
I F Y N S E X K F V A E S N R R W I
S K G A C R R G C U N G Y V E I L N
I A E C O I E C J B E I Z E V A V R
O V R S L N V M F H C O N I X X D D
N B E X L G D Z R B H N N Q Q G U E
O F X Y E X Y M X K O B Q S O S L U
N I K G G W N U D S Q A V V Q K O A
E I Q E E W L U W B K N M T D F J W
V U X J E A W Q X Z U D I E X Q S L
O P T I C A L E N G I N E E R I N G
```

Find These Words

ENGINEERING
VIRGINIA
GREEN
NORFOLK
OPTICALENGINEERING

SPARTANLEGIONBAND
HONORSCOLLEGE
DIVISIONONE
THESPARTANECHO

Directions: Read and answer the questions. These are your opinions so the answers will vary.

Would you rather be famous for an invention or for something you've done?

What's your favorite color?

Share a special memory you have from school.

Directions: Unscramble the words below about NSU. See if you can get the bonus word.

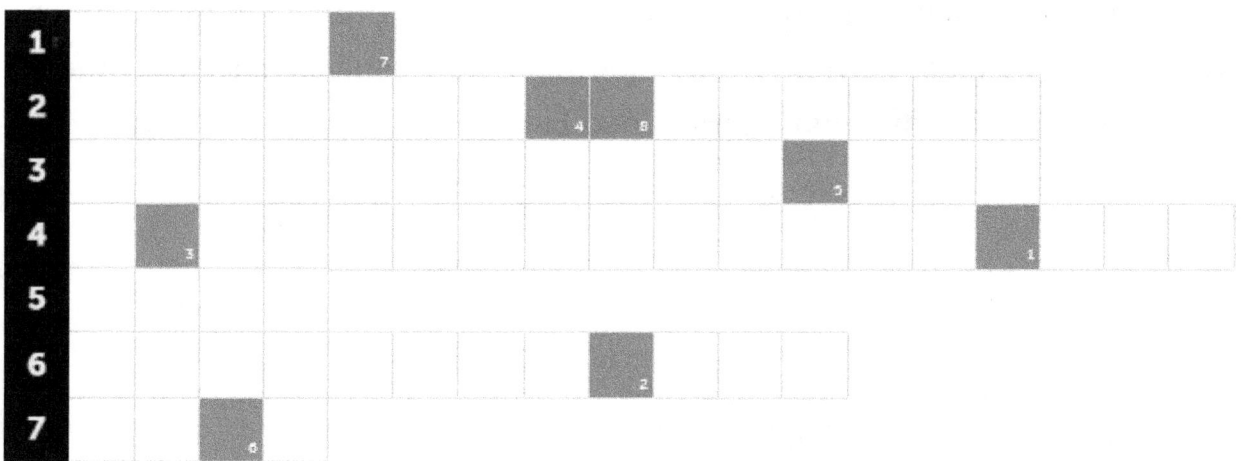

BONUS WORD

1	2	3	4	5	6	7	8

Unscramble Words

1) eenrg
2) euonetercicpcms
3) auiislmtcinrcej
4) -daasuetajovnmasgn
5) ogld
6) raemokmairpl
7) agry

Directions: This is the WGLT Challenge. Solve the cryptogram. As the puzzle solver, you need to find which number belongs to which character. And this can be pretty challenging! You will need to match the number with the letter. There are some letters given to you below. This will help you solve the other words and unlock more characters. **Good Luck.**

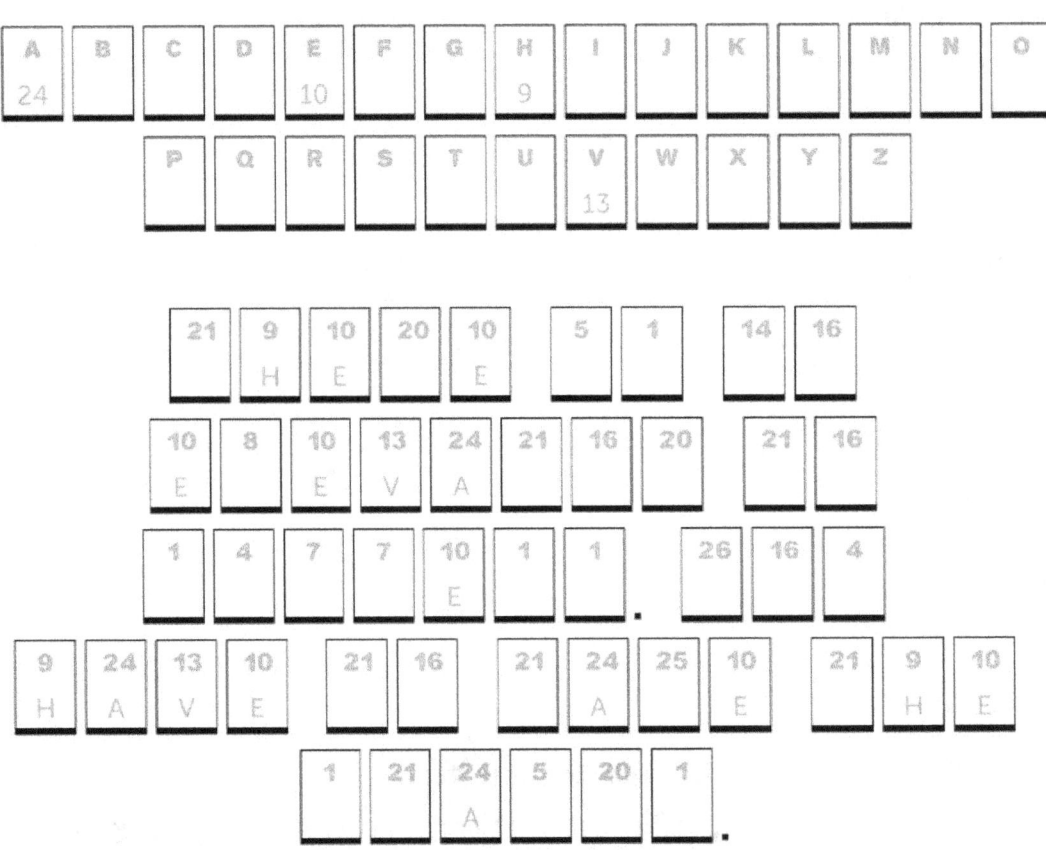

Florida A&M

University

Florida A&M

University

OCTOBER 3, 1887 – PRESENT

LEFT BLANK ON PURPOSE

Florida A&M
University

Florida A&M
University

Directions: read the bio below and answer the following questions.

State Normal College for Colored Students, which is now Florida Agricultural and Mechanical University (FAMU), is a public land-grant HBCU that is dedicated to the advancement of knowledge, the resolution of complex issues and the empowerment of citizens and communities. It was founded on October 3, 1887, in Tallahassee, FL. In 1891, the name was changed to State Normal and Industrial College for Colored Students under the Second Morrill Act. In 1909, the 1905 Buckman Act made the college an official institution of higher learning and the name was changed to Florida Agricultural and Mechanical College for Negroes. In 1953, the name was finally changed to Florida Agricultural and Mechanical University (Florida AGM). Florida AGM is the only surviving publicly funded historically Black college or university in the state of Florida. FAMU is the only public historically Black university in Florida. There are currently three private HBCUs: Bethune-Cookman University, Edward Waters College and Florida Memorial University.

1. This made FAMU an official institution of higher learning?
    A. The Second Morrill Act
    B. The 1905 Buckman Act
    C. The Servicemen's Readjustment Act (GI Bill)
2. What year did FAMU become an university?
    A. 1891
    B. 1953
    C. 1909
3. How many private HBCU's are in the state of Florida?
    A. One
    B. Three
    C. Two

Directions: Answer the questions, to solve the crossword puzzle. You can use the internet if you get stuck on any question.

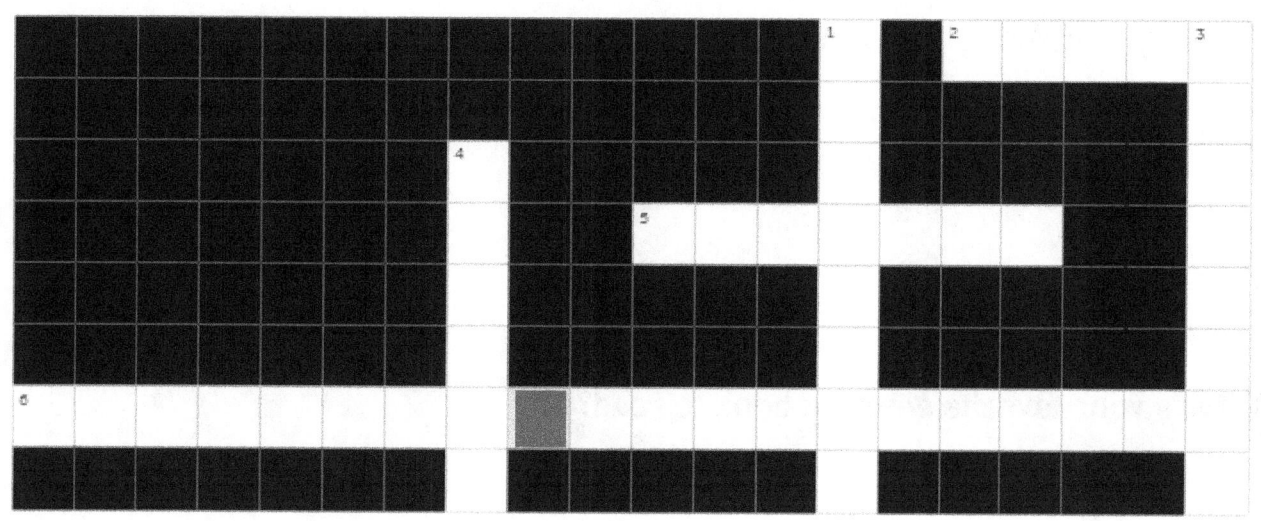

Across

2) FAMU mascot is ____ the Rattlesnake.

5) Samuel H. Coleman Memorial Library is the university's main ____.

6) FAMU has been accredited by the ____ of Colleges and Schools (SACS) since 1935.

Down

1) FAMU started a ____ and nursing program in 1951.

3) FAMU implemented the Medical Scholars Program (MSP) in partnership with the Charles E. Schmidt College of ____.

4) FAMU motto is Excellence With ____.

Directions: Read and answer the questions. These are your opinions so the answers will vary.

Would you rather play an individual or team sport?

What's your favorite genre of book to read?

What goals do you have for yourself? What are 5 things you want to do before you are (21)?

Directions: Unscramble the words below about FAMU. See if you can get the bonus word.

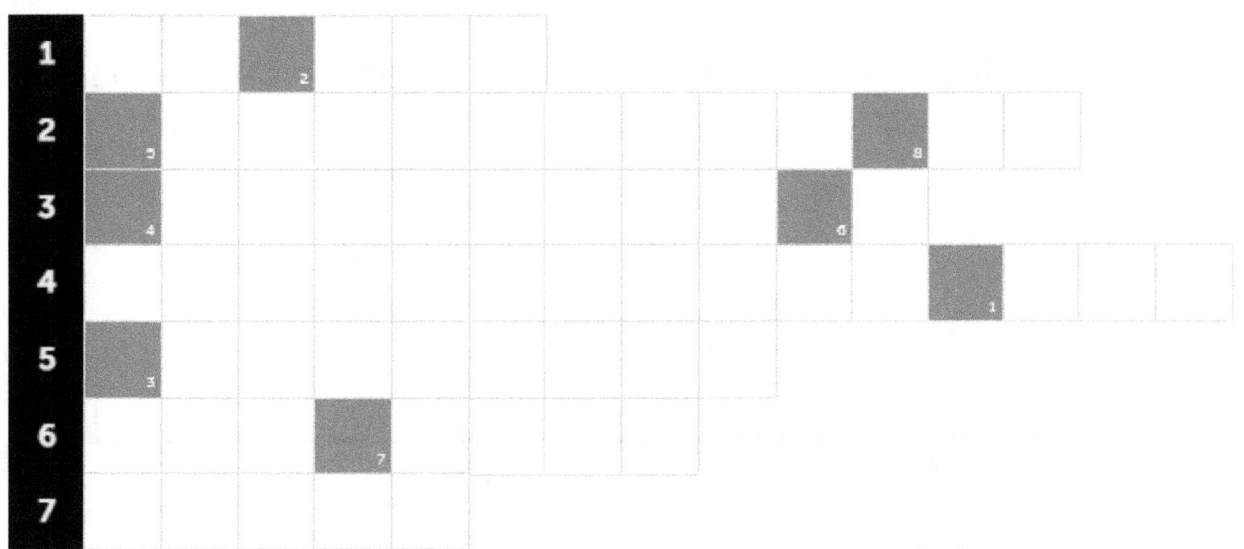

BONUS WORD

Unscramble Words

1) enogar
2) oylnnanrisrro
3) salshaleate
4) eranrblrayicige
5) hatauenmf
6) hacaypmr
7) genre

Directions: This is the WGLT Challenge. Solve the cryptogram. As the puzzle solver, you need to find which number belongs to which character. And this can be pretty challenging! You will need to match the number with the letter. There are some letters given to you below. This will help you solve the other words and unlock more characters. **Good Luck.**

Jackson State
University

Jackson State
University

OCTOBER 23, 1877 – PRESENT

LEFT BLANK ON PURPOSE

Jackson State
University

Jackson State
University

Directions: read the bio below and answer the following questions.

Natchez Seminary, which is now known as Jackson State University (Jackson State or JSU), is a public HBCU that is dedicated to producing technologically advanced, diverse, ethical and global leaders who think critically, address societal problems and compete effectively. It was founded on October 23, 1877, in Natchez, MS by the American Baptist Home Mission Society of NY "for the moral, religious and intellectual improvement of Christian leaders of the colored people of Mississippi and the neighboring states." In 1883, the school changed its name to Jackson College and moved from Natchez to a site in Jackson, MS. In 1940, the school became a state-supported public institution and was known as the Mississippi Negro Training School. In 1944, the name was changed to Jackson College for Negro Teachers to reflect development. In 1967, after desegregation, the name was changed to Jackson State College. In 1974, the name was changed to Jackson State University after the school added graduate programs and expanded its curriculum.

1. **What city did JSU start in?**
   A. Clinton, MS
   B. Jackson, MS
   C. Natchez, MS
2. **What year did Natchez Seminary become a college?**
   A. 1940
   B. 1944
   C. 1967
3. **Which acronym represents Jackson State University?**
   A. JSCC
   B. JSU
   C. JSS

Directions: Find the words associated with Jackson State University.

N	P	N	A	D	G	O	K	N	R	J	S	H	P	C	C	X	E	N
M	P	X	Q	J	N	E	J	S	Q	F	F	X	H	O	V	D	A	U
C	A	U	X	X	T	N	V	G	R	H	W	A	V	G	S	V	T	D
L	B	W	E	B	D	U	B	O	I	S	N	G	W	D	Y	X	I	K
C	W	W	Q	O	H	O	T	O	N	G	V	E	N	B	G	K	G	K
I	G	P	S	K	O	F	T	O	I	W	W	I	L	N	U	S	E	R
V	R	I	P	K	X	Y	H	N	J	K	M	U	I	L	B	N	R	U
I	K	R	W	F	M	L	G	H	N	G	E	R	L	F	Y	M	B	Y
L	Y	D	G	Z	U	L	S	I	N	A	E	X	E	N	F	Z	A	K
R	G	C	F	A	I	E	E	I	N	E	Y	Z	T	M	A	O	T	K
I	K	Z	I	V	X	P	G	D	N	O	Z	L	T	J	Y	R	T	G
G	H	A	E	Z	B	N	W	I	T	V	L	Z	R	F	S	I	A	Z
H	J	S	Y	G	E	H	G	Q	H	L	U	Q	H	R	V	F	L	S
T	V	A	K	L	I	N	E	I	P	W	J	K	E	S	C	T	I	D
S	L	C	L	T	E	M	S	H	J	Z	D	G	E	E	I	O	O	N
O	J	A	E	F	R	N	G	L	M	L	I	H	B	O	L	R	N	X
M	H	I	O	A	G	T	X	I	L	T	S	M	X	J	Z	X	P	Q
C	M	Q	D	Z	M	J	W	A	G	Z	N	W	A	A	V	S	C	T
S	O	N	I	C	B	O	O	M	O	F	T	H	E	S	O	U	T	H

Find These Words

WEBDUBOIS
NAVYBLUEANDWHITE
CHANGINGLIVES
TIGERBATTALION
TIGERS

ENGINEERING
CHALLENGINGMINDS
CIVILRIGHTS
SONICBOOMOFTHESOUTH

Directions: Read and answer the questions. These are your opinions so the answers will vary.

Would you rather text your friends or get together?

What's your favorite story about your life so far?

Describe a situation where you showed extra kindness toward a stranger/friend.

Directions: Unscramble the words below about JSU. See if you can get the bonus word.

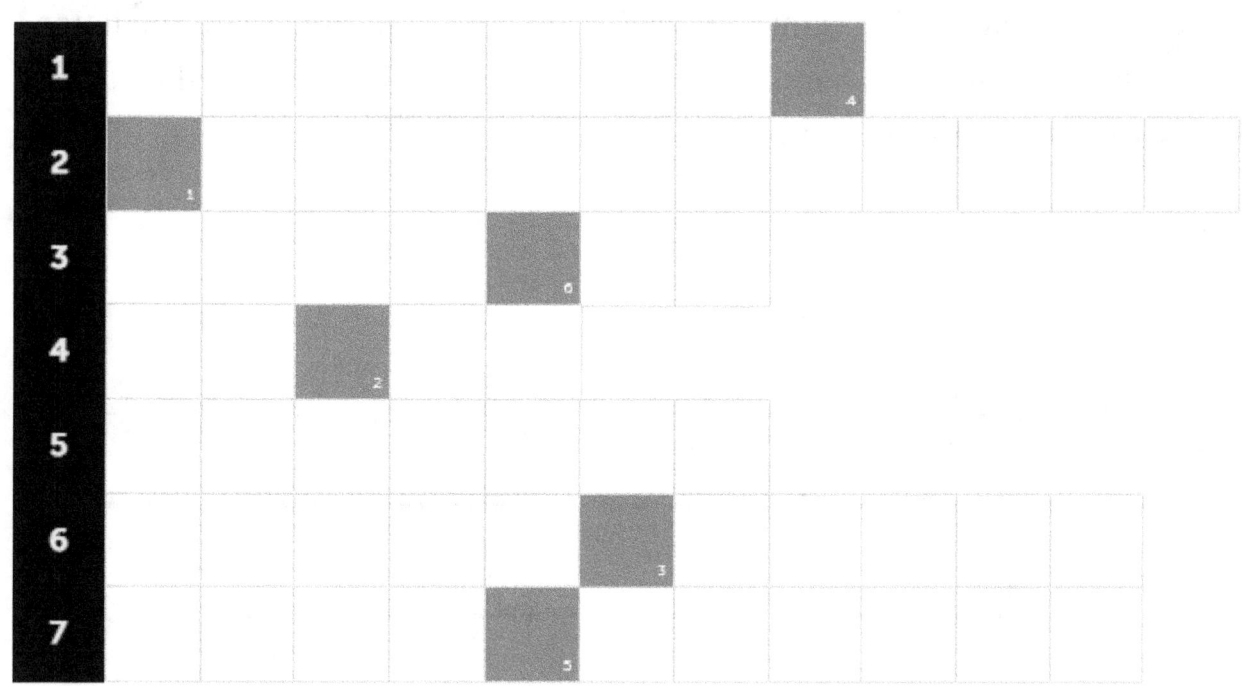

BONUS WORD

Unscramble Words

1) yanubevl   **2)** ushsmhodatno   **3)** jascnok
4) hweit   **5)** tncaehx   **6)** gunfodlcele
7) btrilaaresl

113

Directions: This is the WGLT Challenge. Solve the cryptogram. As the puzzle solver, you need to find which number belongs to which character. And this can be pretty challenging! You will need to match the number with the letter. There are some letters given to you below. This will help you solve the other words and unlock more characters. **Good Luck.**

North Carolina A&T

State University

North Carolina A&T

State University

MARCH 9, 1891 – PRESENT

North Carolina A&T

State University

North Carolina A&T

State University

Directions: read the bio below and answer the following questions.

Agricultural and Mechanical College for the Colored Race, which is now called North Carolina Agricultural and Technical State University (also known as North Carolina AGT State University, North Carolina AGT, N.C. AGT, or simply AGT), is a public HBCU that is dedicated to creating innovative solutions that address the challenges and economic needs of North Carolina, the nation and the world. It was founded on March 9, 1891, in Raleigh, NC. Due to the Second Morrill Act, which required that each state demonstrate that race was not an admissions criterion or else designate a separate land-grant institution for persons of color, the North Carolina General Assembly established the college as an annex of the private Shaw University in Raleigh. In 1892, the college was moved to Greensboro, NC. In 1915, the North Carolina General Assembly changed the name of the college to Negro Agricultural and Technical College of North Carolina. In 1957, the college changed its name again to Agricultural and Technical College of North Carolina.

1. Which acronym is for North Carolina A&T ?
    A. UNC
    B. NCSU
    C. N.C. A&T
2. What year did A&T move to Greensboro, NC?
    A. 1892
    B. 1891
    C. 1893
3. What does A&T stand for in the college name?
    A. Agricultural and Technology
    B. Administrative and Technical
    C. Agricultural and Technical

Directions: Answer the questions, to solve the crossword puzzle. You can use the internet if you get stuck on any question.

Across
3) N.C. A&T mascot is Aggie the _____.
5) N.C. A&T galleries are home to the Mattye Reed _____ and the H. Clinton Taylor Collections.
6) N.C. A&T first ___ was John Oliver Crosby.

Down
1) N.C. A&T offers 54 undergraduate, 29 master's and nine ____ degrees through its eight colleges.
2) Some of N.C. A&T track and field team went on to represent the United States at the 2020 ____, where they captured 3 medals, 2 of them being gold.
4) N.C. A&T is a member of the Southeastern Universities Research Association and classified by the ____ Foundation as a doctoral-granting high research activity university.

Directions: Read and answer the questions. These are your opinions so the answers will vary.

Would you rather be a wizard or a superhero?

What's your favorite video game?

Why do you think it is important to have rules in school?

Directions: Unscramble the words below about N.C. A&T. See if you can get the bonus word.

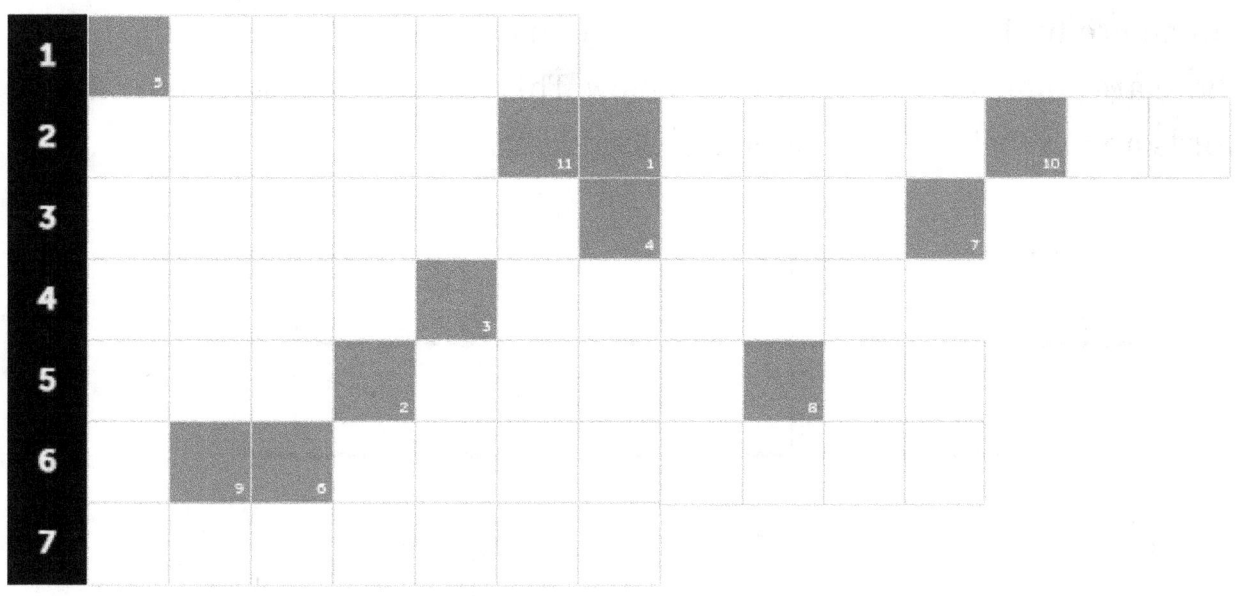

BONUS WORD

Unscramble Words

1) sgieag
2) ltraiomsrarndh
3) danuellgdbo
4) negrbeosor
5) ivlcgishitr
6) icneenoacns
7) ngbwlio

Directions: This is the WGLT Challenge. Solve the cryptogram. As the puzzle solver, you need to find which number belongs to which character. And this can be pretty challenging! You will need to match the number with the letter. There are some letters given to you below. This will help you solve the other words and unlock more characters. **Good Luck.**

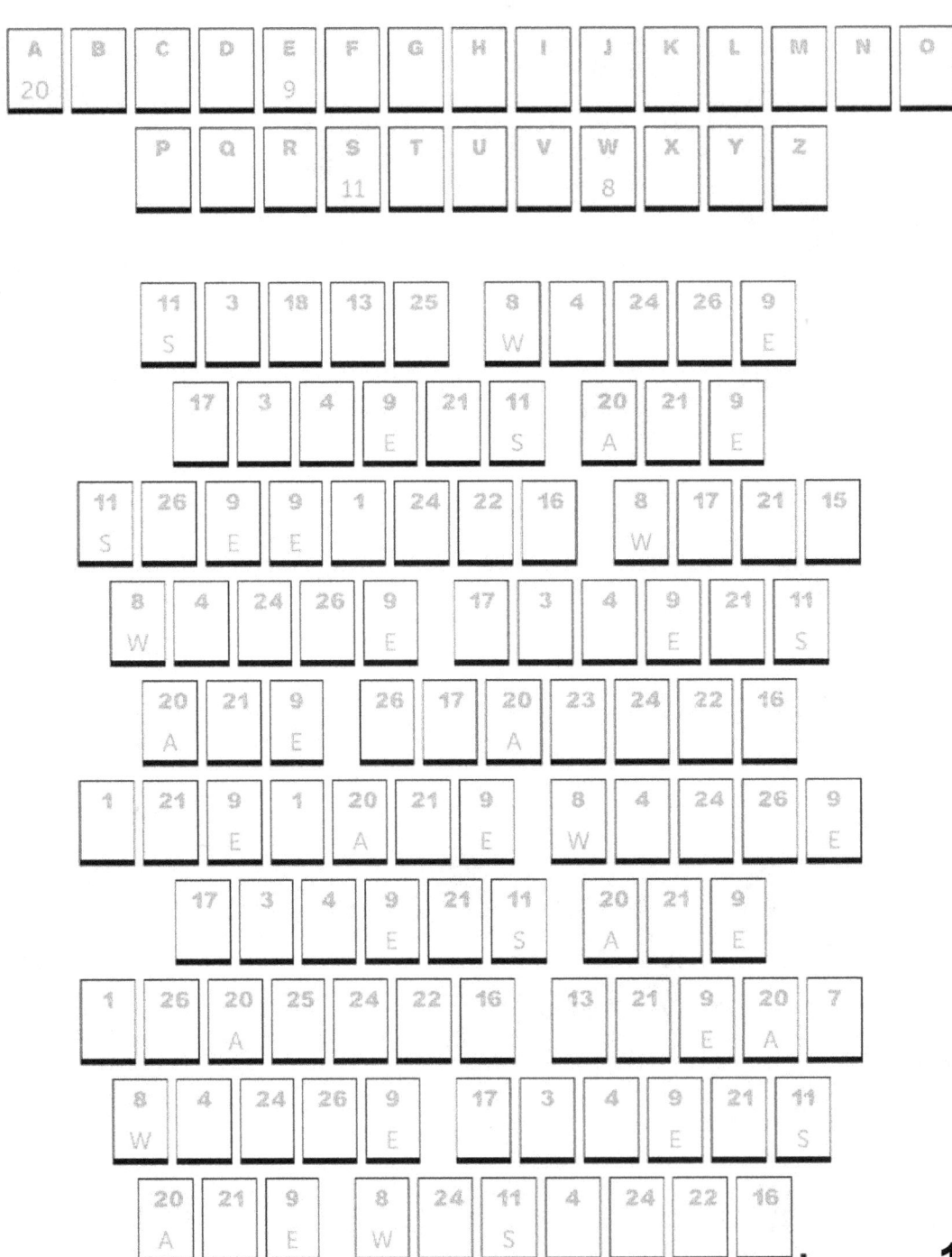

122

Clark Atlanta

University

Clark Atlanta

University

SEPTEMBER 19, 1865 – PRESENT

LEFT BLANK ON PURPOSE

Clark Atlanta

University

Clark Atlanta

University

Directions: read the bio below and answer the following questions.

Atlanta University, which is now Clark Atlanta University (CAU or Clark Atlanta), is a private Methodist HBCU that is dedicated to providing academic excellence, building character and encouraging service to others. It was founded on September 19, 1865, in Atlanta, GA. Atlanta University was the nation's first graduate institution to award degrees to African Americans in the nation and the first to award bachelor's degrees to African Americans in the South. In 1869, Clark University, which was then called Clark College, was founded by the Methodist Episcopal Church, which later became the United Methodist Church and was the nation's first four-year liberal arts college to serve a primarily African American student population. Clark College was named after Bishop Davis Wasgatt Clark, who was the first president of the Freedman's Aid Society and became a bishop in 1864. In 1929, the Atlanta University Affiliation was established and Atlanta University became a graduate school. In 1988, Atlanta University merged with Clark College and the two became Clark Atlanta University.

1. Which college was founded by the Methodist Church?
   A. Atlanta University
   B. Clark College
   C. Clark Atlanta Univeristy
2. What year did Atlanta and Clark merge together?
   A. 1929
   B. 1988
   C. 1869
3. What did Atlanta University do first in the South?
   A. Be the first HBCU
   B. Become an all male college
   C. Award a Bachelor's degree to African-American

Directions: Find the words associated with Clark Atlanta University.

```
D O C T O R A L U N I V E R I S I T Y
I Z L C K I J Q N H J L R Z T P W J C
J P K J D N A B R E H T A P N H C G R
Z X I V N V R Y U E F Z A A M I L C S
P K Z N R I E P D D D X K S U L K D P
E A V W D O D J E C A I K A X A - Q A
C N V F K O - M U B P A M Y Y N J V C
N D N F K M B H I P D C L N Z T A W E
E M N C I S L I V A A G Z J H H Z K G
I X Z U P I A C M Z W Q C L A R Z R R
C X S Z U W C A P A O F S T D O - W A
S B U G V I K N W Y A B N N G P R K N
D P S Y G W - Z O E H A W D E Y A G T
N G J V X I G O Z E L O E H G T D R U
A L Y R Z O R Q D T Z C S G T F I A D
S D C K W B A J A N J P S P F V O G J
T B S I X S Y Y Q G V E U R P I T Z Q
R U J V E N O - E K A M S L O C Q C S
A D G H O F S R R A F K Q H W K J C X
```

Find These Words

PHILANTHROPY   RED-BLACK-GRAY
ATLANTA   SPACEGRANT
DOCTORALUNIVERISITY   ARTSANDSCIENCE
PATHERBAND   WCLK-JAZZ-RADIO
MAKE-ONE

Directions: Read and answer the questions. These are your opinions so the answers will vary.

Would you rather play hide-and-seek or dodgeball?

What's your favorite subject in school?

What is one rule in all schools that you feel is unfair?

Directions: Unscramble the words below about CAU. See if you can get the bonus word.

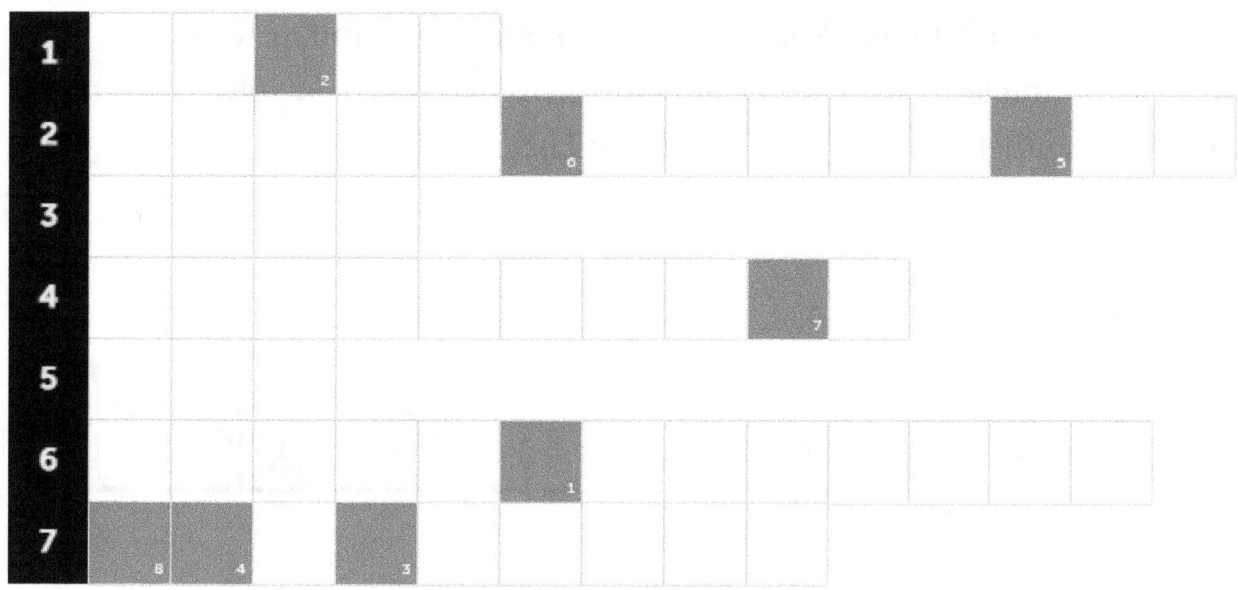

BONUS WORD

Unscramble Words

1) Balck
2) ejgneghfrrocre
3) rgay
4) okriacolws
5) rde
6) axpenrceiueec
7) onestlhea

Directions: This is the WGLT Challenge. Solve the cryptogram. As the puzzle solver, you need to find which number belongs to which character. And this can be pretty challenging! You will need to match the number with the letter. There are some letters given to you below. This will help you solve the other words and unlock more characters. **Good Luck.**

130

JANUARY 9, 1866 – PRESENT

LEFT BLANK ON PURPOSE

Fisk University

Fisk University

Fisk University

Fisk University

Fisk University

Fisk University

Directions: read the bio below and answer the following questions.

Fisk Free Colored School, which is now known as Fisk University is a private HBCU that is dedicated to producing graduates from diverse backgrounds with the integrity and intellect required for making substantive contributions to society. It was founded on January 9, 1866, in Nashville, TN, by John Ogden, Erastus Milo Cravath and Edward Parmelee Smith of the American Missionary Association for the Education of Freedmen in Nashville. The school was named after Clinton B. Fisk, who was a Union general. In 1867, the Fisk Free Colored School was renamed Fisk University. In 1875, James Burrus and Virginia Walker graduated from Fisk and became the first African American students to graduate from a liberal arts college south of the Mason-Dixon line. In 1930, Fisk University became the first African American institution to gain accreditation from the Southern Association of Colleges and Schools (SACS). Fisk University is the oldest HBCU in Nashville.

1. What association is Fisk University apart of?
   A. South Florida Manufacturers Association
   B. State Societies in the Southeast
   C. Southern Association of Colleges and Schools
2. What rank was Clinton Fisk?
   A. Colonel
   B. General
   C. Major
3. Fisk is the ___ higher education institution in Nashville?
   A. Oldest University
   B. Oldest HBCU
   C. Oldest College

Directions: Answer the questions, to solve the crossword puzzle. You can use the internet if you get stuck on any question.

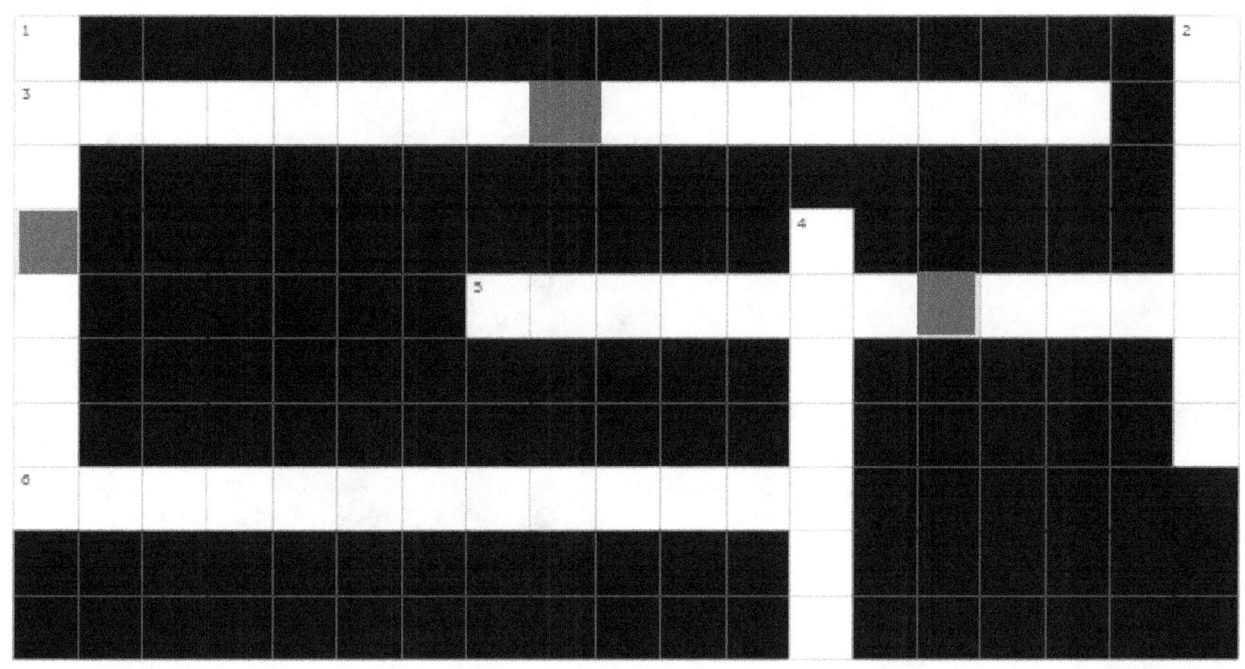

Across
3) Fisk University is designated as a National ____.
5) ____, the South's first permanent structure built for the education of black students.
6) Fisk University was the first African-American institution to gain ____ by the Southern Association of Colleges and Schools.

Down
1) Fisk University has a chapter of ____ Kappa the nation's oldest and most widely known academic honor society.
2) Fisk University was the home to the world-famous ____ Singers.
4) Fisk University first students ranged in age from seven to ____.

Directions: Read and answer the questions. These are your opinions so the answers will vary.

Would you rather eat at home or in a restaurant?

What's your favorite activity to do with friends?

Do peers deserve the same respect as elders? Why?

Directions: Unscramble the words below about Fisk University. See if you can get the bonus word.

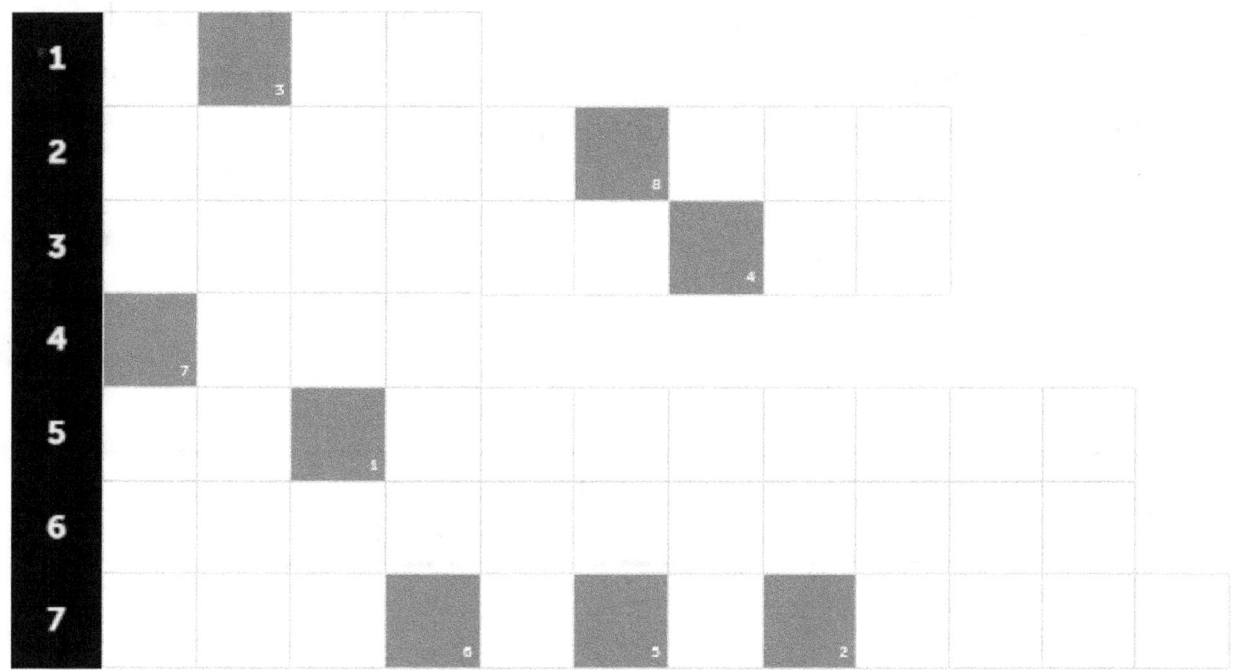

BONUS WORD

Unscramble Words

1) lbeu
2) ikrssnfam
3) nhaesvill
4) odlg
5) jlebilhuela
6) irlhsvigcit
7) raloasodguan

Directions: This is the WGLT Challenge. Solve the cryptogram. As the puzzle solver, you need to find which number belongs to which character. And this can be pretty challenging! You will need to match the number with the letter. There are some letters given to you below. This will help you solve the other words and unlock more characters. **Good Luck.**

SEPTEMBER 13, 1886 – PRESENT

LEFT BLANK ON PURPOSE

University Of
Maryland Eastern
Shore

University Of
Maryland Eastern
Shore

Directions: read the bio below and answer the following questions.

Delaware Conference Academy, which is now called the University of Maryland Eastern Shore (UMES), is a public land-grant HBCU that is dedicated to a holistic learning environment that fosters multicultural diversity, academic success and intellectual and social growth. It was founded on September 13, 1886, in Princess Anne, MD. In 1890, it changed its name to Morgan College to honor the first chairman of its board of trustees, Rev. Lyttleton Morgan. In 1919, the Land-Grant Program for Blacks assumed control of the Princess Anne Academy and renamed it the Eastern Shore Branch of the Maryland Agricultural College. In 1948, the Eastern Shore Branch of Maryland was renamed Maryland State College and became a division of the University of Maryland. In 1970, Maryland State College became the University of Maryland Eastern Shore. It is a part of the University System of Maryland public institutions of higher education.

1. Which name came from a member of trustees?
   A. Princess Anne Academy
   B. Morgan College
   C. Maryland State College
2. What year UMES become an University?
   A. 1970
   B. 1948
   C. 1919
3. What was UMES original name?
   A. Maryland State College
   B. Princess Anne Academy
   C. Delaware Conference Academy

Directions: Find the words associated with UMES.

```
L G S C P L Z M A I W T P V Q M I G
F F X Q P P P A M Q L T R K T G U T
S W C Y X B V B H Y A X B M X P H R
U O V D W F J Z K Q G I K G G E X H
M M B W Z V H I Q Y A G V X - K U U
M E H D Q F X L A H I F R A O Q Z H
E N C N N X P I B T X T R N L P A G
R S T U D M D T S H E T Y O F Y B R
O - D F G N L V H O S F B D F H K R
L B I E K W A H E H T Y R R A H Z H
Y O B G S E M L H F B T U Z M E K D
M W L E K W P N Y A E F K T A M W Q
P L J L W C M K L R D P G S R P W N
I I A L A M X I S A A N J F O L R G
C N B O H L Y D N L Z M G P O Q F O
S G M C T C O P X B L W S Z N W D A
D I W U J R M F O N T F Z T L P T G
H U B E N N A - S S E C N I R P A I
```

Find These Words

HARRYTHEHAWK   PRINCESS-ANNE   HAWKS
MAROON   THE-ARTS   WOMENS-BOWLING
SUMMEROLYMPICS   COLLEGEFUND   MARYLAND

Directions: Read and answer the questions. These are your opinions so the answers will vary.

Would you rather visit the mountains or the ocean?

What's your favorite show on TV?

How do you prefer others show kindness- hugs, notes, time together, etc?

Directions: Unscramble the words below about UMES. See if you can get the bonus word.

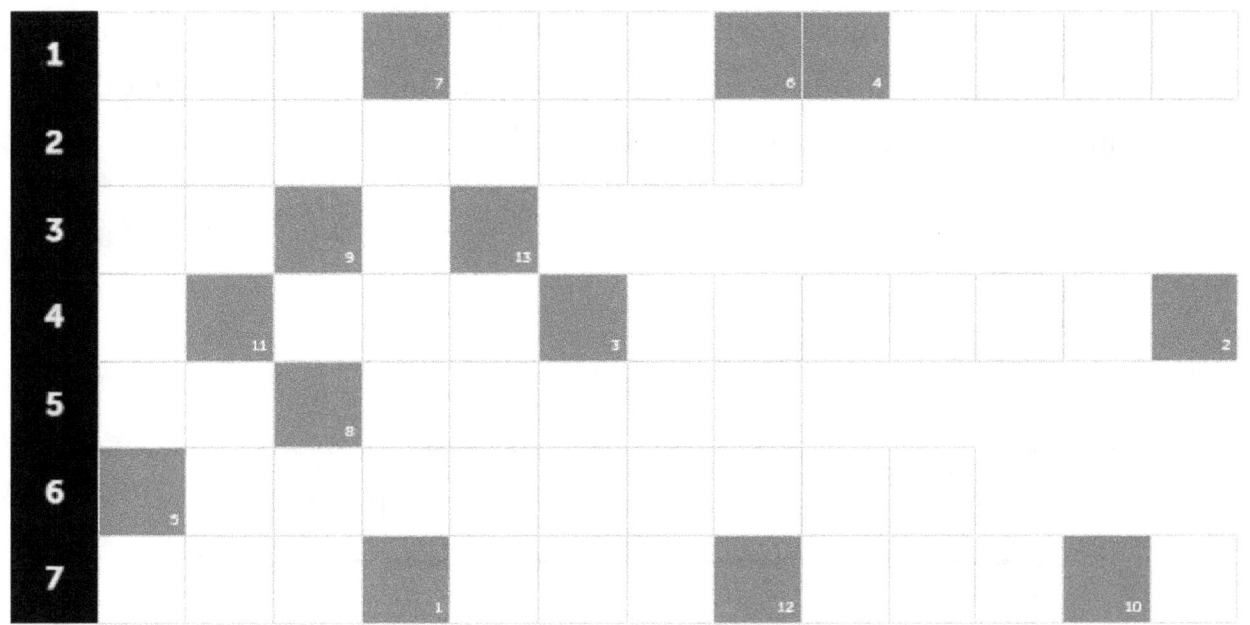

BONUS WORD

Unscramble Words

1) oonarngmydaar
2) aarhypcm
3) wkhsa
4) -ssiapncnneer
5) htsellra
6) canresaptg
7) esodiihadennr

Directions: This is the WGLT Challenge. Solve the cryptogram. As the puzzle solver, you need to find which number belongs to which character. And this can be pretty challenging! You will need to match the number with the letter. There are some letters given to you below. This will help you solve the other words and unlock more characters. **Good Luck.**

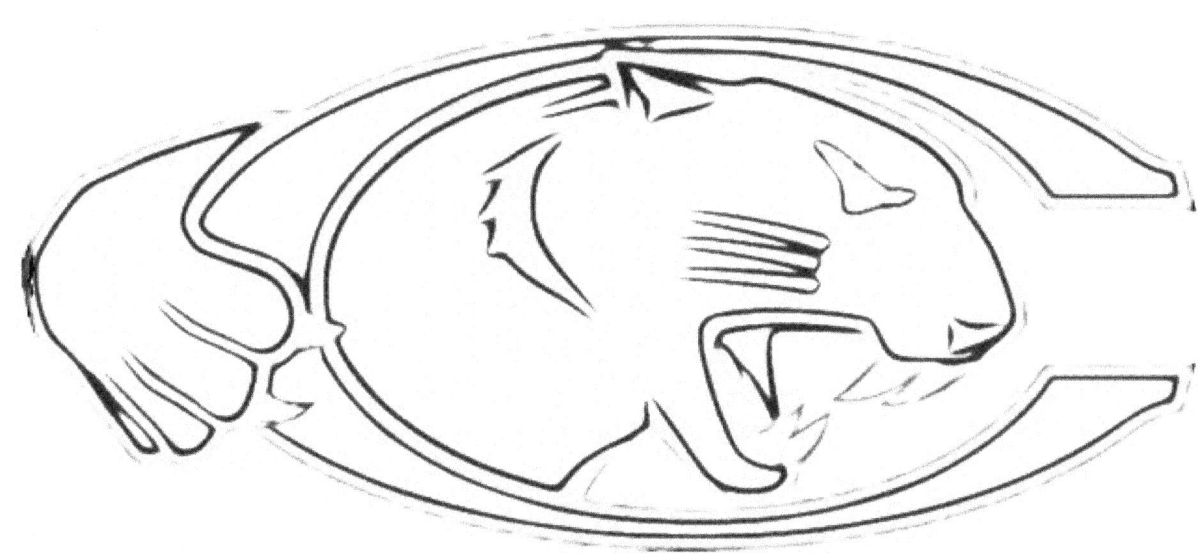

1869 – PRESENT

LEFT BLANK ON PURPOSE

Claflin University

Claflin University

Claflin University

Claflin University

Claflin University

Claflin University

Directions: read the bio below and answer the following questions.

Claflin University is a private HBCU that is dedicated to providing a student-centered liberal arts education that is grounded in cutting-edge research, experiential learning, state-of-the-art technology, community service and life-long personal and professional fulfillment. It was founded in 1869 in Orangeburg, SC, by Alonzo Webster, who was a minister from Vermont who had come to South Carolina to teach at the Baker Bible Institute, which trained African American ministers for the Methodist Episcopal Church. In 1869, Webster received a charter from the state of South Carolina to establish a college that would prepare freed slaves for the responsibilities of citizenship. Claflin University was named in honor of Lee Claflin, who was a philanthropist and prominent Methodist layman from Boston and his son William Claflin, who was then the governor of Massachusetts. Claflin is the oldest HBCU in South Carolina and touts itself as the first college in the state to welcome all students regardless of race or gender.

1. Who was Claflin University named after?
   A. Lee Claflin
   B. Alonzo Webster
   C. William Claflin
2. Claflin was the first college to do what in SC?
   A. Have an Medical department
   B. Accept all students regardless of race or gender
   C. Graduate a male and female
3. Claflin is the oldest HBCU in?
   A. North Carolina
   B. South Dakota
   C. South Carolina

Directions: Answer the questions, to solve the crossword puzzle. You can use the internet if you get stuck on any question.

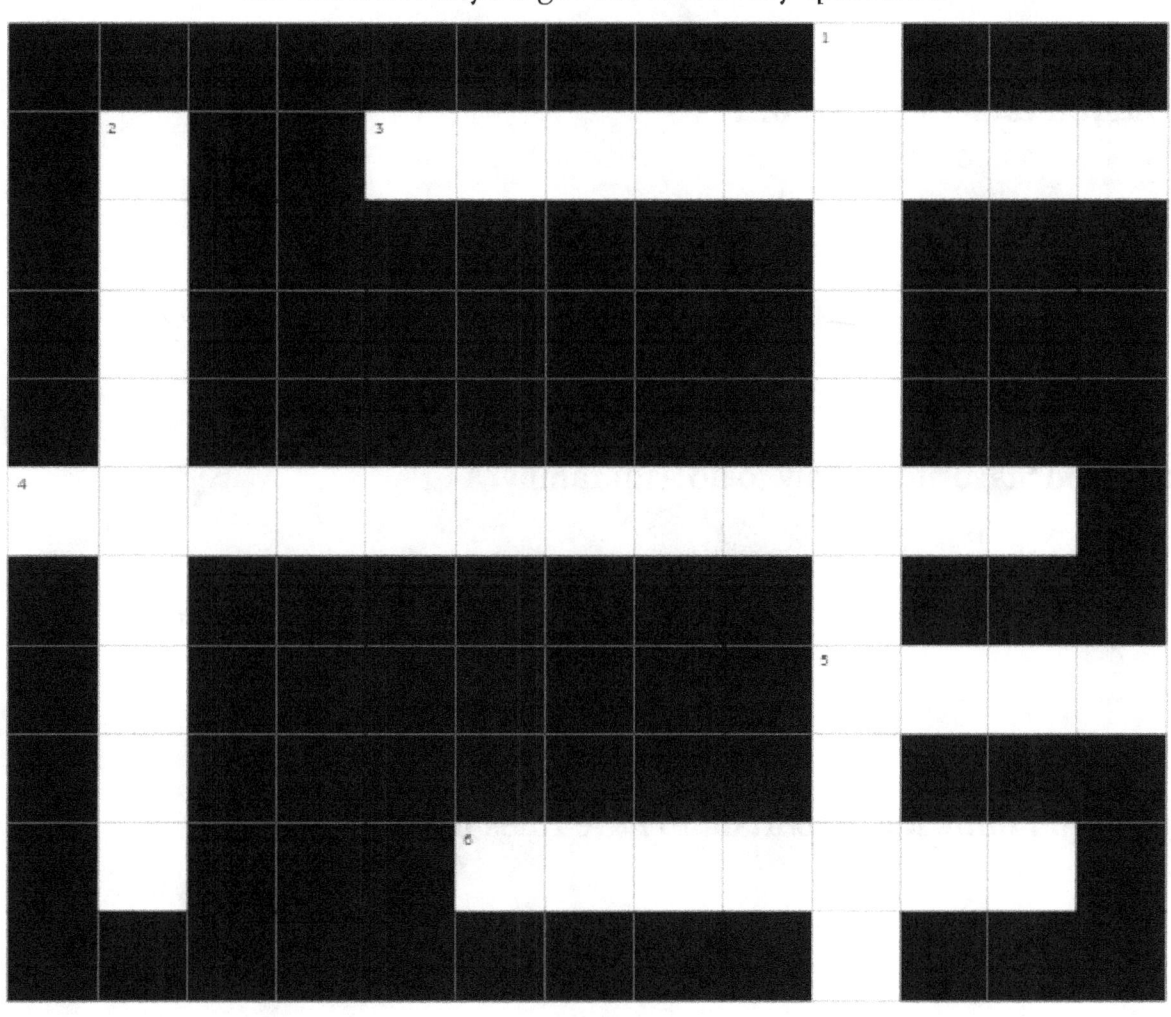

Across

3) Claflin University has produced students who have been named Pickering and _____ scholars.

4) Claflin University graduates who complete the R.O.T.C. program may be _____ as second lieutenants in the U.S. Army.

5) Claflin University says that they are the first college in the state to welcome all students regardless of ____ or gender.

6) Claflin University use to be called Claflin ____ in 1979.

Down

1) Claflin University's motto is; "The World Needs _____."

2) Claflin University was named after two _____ churchmen: Governor William Claflin and his father, Lee Claflin

Directions: Read and answer the questions. These are your opinions so the answers will vary.

Would you rather have art or PE?

What's your favorite activity to do with family?

Why do you think it is important to have rules in society?

Directions: Unscramble the words below about Claflin University. See if you can get the bonus word.

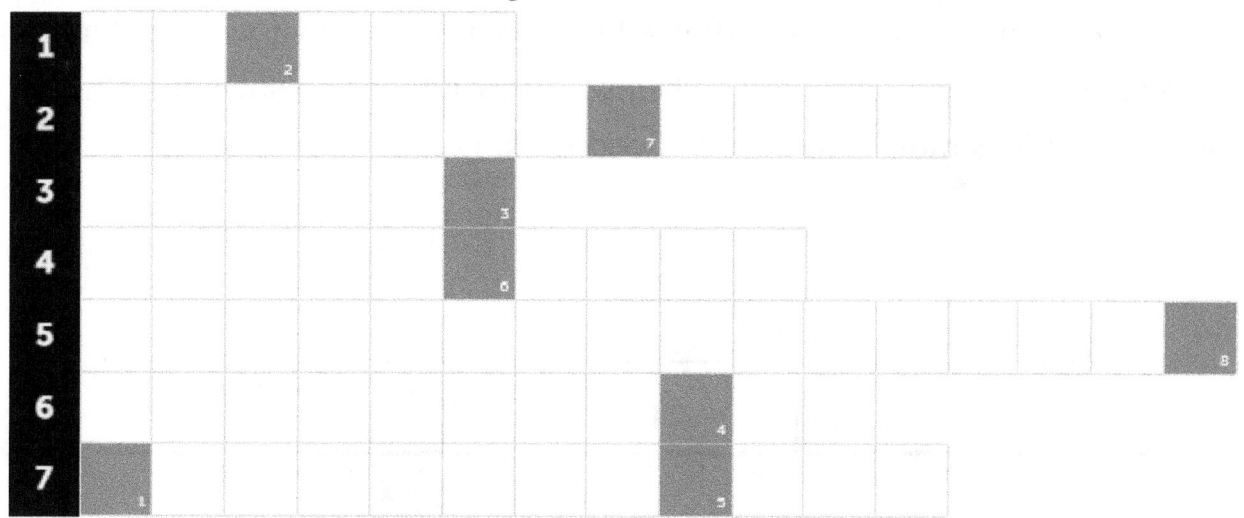

BONUS WORD

1	2	3	4	5	6	7	8

Unscramble Words

1) oneagr
2) anwwacurdkma
3) onmroa
4) grrbagoune
5) ntesaeuncl-crsai
6) brbertaotse
7) cu-vripteabh

Directions: This is the WGLT Challenge. Solve the cryptogram. As the puzzle solver, you need to find which number belongs to which character. And this can be pretty challenging! You will need to match the number with the letter. There are some letters given to you below. This will help you solve the other words and unlock more characters. **Good Luck.**

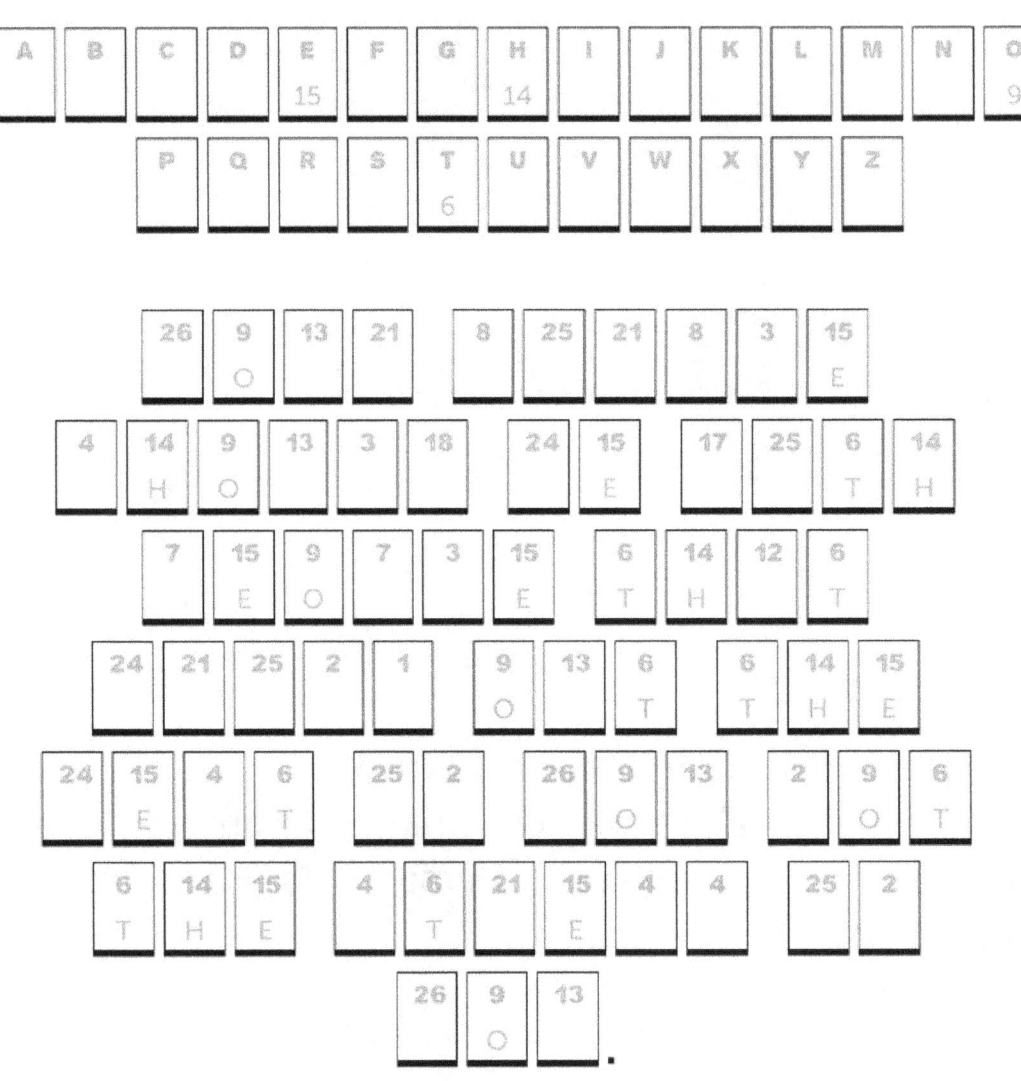

Solution:

YOUR CIRCLE SHOULD BE WITH PEOPLE THAT BRING OUT THE BEST IN YOU NOT THE STRESS IN YOU.

Winston Salem

State University

Winston Salem

State University

SEPTEMBER 28, 1892 – PRESENT

Winston Salem

State University

Winston Salem

State University

Directions: read the bio below and answer the following questions.

Slater Industrial Academy, which is now Winston-Salem State University (WSSU), is a public HBCU that is dedicated to the holistic development of students by faculty who are dedicated to excellence in teaching, research and service. It was founded on September 28, 1892, in Winston-Salem, NC. In 1899, Slater Industrial Academy was chartered by the state as Slater Industrial and Slater Normal School. In 1925, the North Carolina General Assembly renamed the school Winston-Salem Teachers College and the North Carolina State Board of Education allowed the college to award elementary teacher education degrees, which made it the first Black institution to provide this specialized training. In 1963, the name was changed from Winston-Salem Teachers College to Winston-Salem State College and was changed again in 1969 to Winston-Salem State University. WSSU is also a part of the University of North Carolina.

1. Which name did WSSU start off with?
    A. Winston-Salem Teachers College
    B. Winston-Salem State College
    C. Slater Industrial Academy
2. What year did WSSC become a University?
    A. 1963
    B. 1969
    C. 1925
3. What was WSSU the first HBCU to do?
    A. Offer a Bachelors degree
    B. Offer specialized training
    C. Offer a Associates degree

Directions: Find the words associated with WSSU.

A	D	E	P	A	R	T	-	T	O	-	S	E	R	V	E	J	B
H	A	C	O	K	E	L	L	Y	-	L	I	B	R	A	R	Y	A
E	E	Y	W	I	N	S	T	O	N	-	S	A	L	E	M	G	K
S	N	A	W	C	I	B	V	H	D	B	P	M	K	I	E	Y	E
Z	E	T	L	W	J	M	H	R	X	N	O	E	M	P	O	F	T
F	R	J	E	T	E	Q	I	A	N	S	Z	W	Z	Z	Z	O	Z
K	N	N	Y	R	H	J	U	M	Y	E	K	R	S	H	T	S	Q
I	R	A	R	P	-	-	U	S	N	M	M	N	V	D	P	U	B
B	R	Y	Q	J	K	T	S	O	R	A	P	H	N	P	Z	J	X
T	C	E	G	E	L	L	O	C	-	S	R	E	H	C	A	E	T
F	L	N	S	N	Z	F	U	-	I	V	T	G	A	Q	W	R	O
L	I	F	E	L	O	N	G	-	L	E	A	R	N	I	N	G	J
I	J	Z	N	Q	G	E	K	O	U	E	N	D	D	M	H	A	N
P	L	E	N	X	A	A	Q	B	G	P	A	C	T	J	A	K	N
J	A	C	V	S	Z	X	L	N	N	G	M	R	E	R	T	E	Z
K	O	D	I	N	W	C	W	P	R	S	T	N	N	S	S	X	M
S	C	A	R	L	E	T	T	A	N	D	W	H	I	T	E	P	Y
S	O	V	O	K	L	X	P	J	A	Q	C	Y	D	T	U	F	K

Find These Words

LIFELONG-LEARNING
RAMS
ENTER-TO-LEARN
WINSTON-SALEM
OKELLY-LIBRARY

HEALTH-SCIENCES
SCARLETTANDWHITE
DEPART-TO-SERVE
TEACHERS-COLLEGE

Directions: Read and answer the questions. These are your opinions so the answers will vary.

If you could travel anywhere in our solar system, where would you go?

What's your favorite meal of the day?

Have you volunteered in your community?

Directions: Unscramble the words below about WSSU. See if you can get the bonus word.

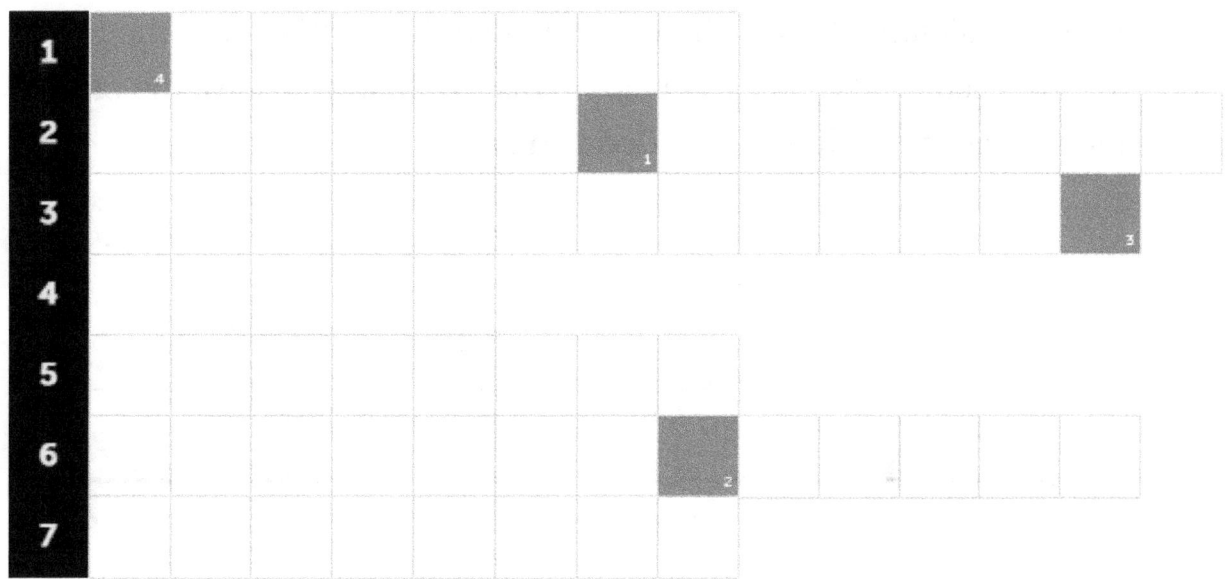

BONUS WORD

Unscramble Words

1) clatrets
2) nowodbeisronlo
3) itwnaoe-mslns
4) thiwe
5) eiensscc
6) li-ggrdlasyge
7) gclkyole

Directions: This is the WGLT Challenge. Solve the cryptogram. As the puzzle solver, you need to find which number belongs to which character. And this can be pretty challenging! You will need to match the number with the letter. There are some letters given to you below. This will help you solve the other words and unlock more characters. **Good Luck.**

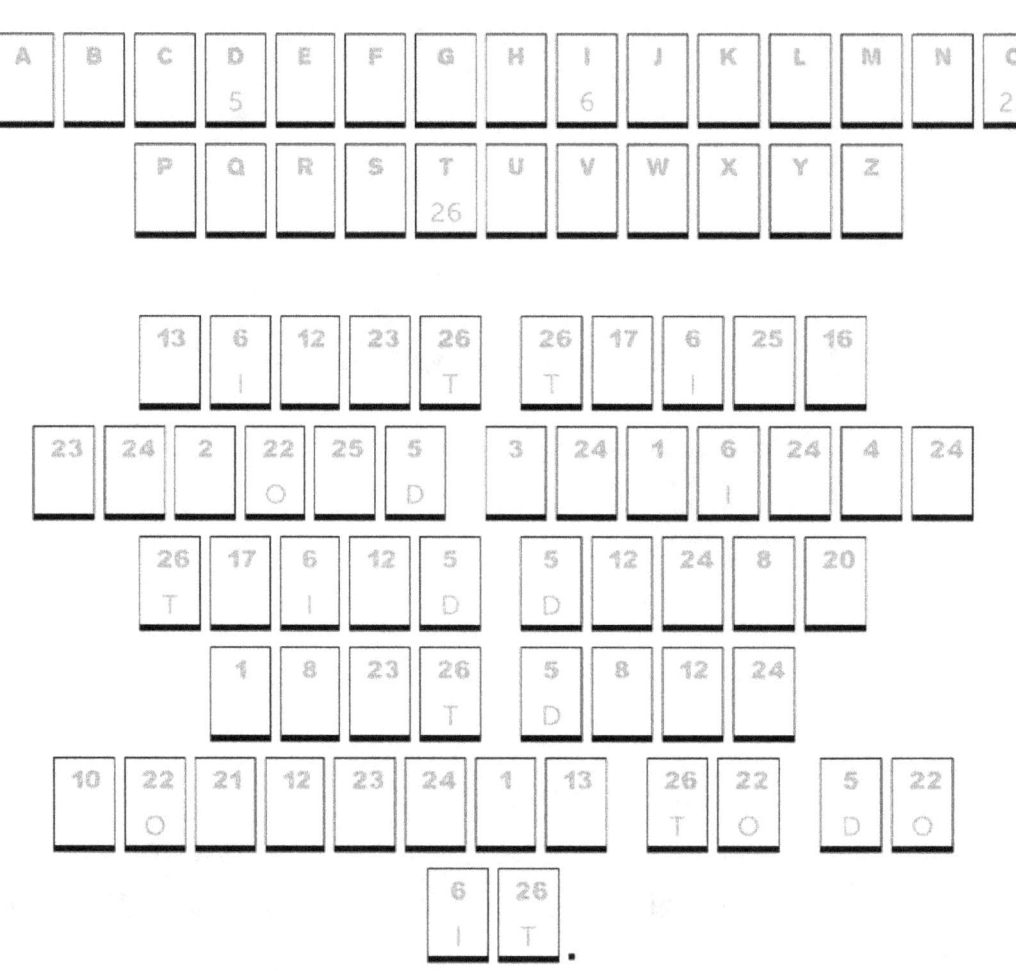

Delaware State

University

Delaware State

University

MAY 15, 1891 – PRESENT

Delaware State
University

Delaware State
University

Directions: read the bio below and answer the following questions.

Delaware College for Colored Students, which is now called Delaware State University (DSU or Del State), is a public land-grant HBCU that is dedicated to providing meaningful and relevant education that emphasizes both the liberal and professional assets of higher education to the people of Delaware and others who are admitted. It was founded on May 15, 1891, in Dover, DE. In 1893, the state changed the school's name to State College for Colored Students to eliminate any confusion with Delaware College. In 1947, the name was changed again to Delaware State College (DSC). In 1993, DSC changed its name to Delaware State University (DSU). In 2021, DSU officially acquired Wesley College, which was a 157-year-old private institution that was founded by the Methodist Church in 1873. This acquisition made DSU the first HBCU to acquire an institution that was not an HBCU. The university has renamed the former Wesley campus "DSU Downtown" and has relocated some of its College of Health and Behavioral Science divisions there.

1. Which name was changed to stop confusion in the state?
    A. State College for Colored Students
    B. Delaware College
    C. Delaware College for Colored Students
2. What year did DSU become an university?
    A. 1947
    B. 1993
    C. 1893
3. DSU was the first HBCU to do what?
    A. Acquire an land-grant from the state
    B. Acquire an HBCU
    C. Acquire an institution that is not a HBCU

Directions: Answer the questions, to solve the crossword puzzle. You can use the internet if you get stuck on any question.

Across

3) Delaware State University has over thirty formal ____ partnerships with institutions in countries like Egypt, France and Italy.

4) Delaware State University has a ____ hall dedicated to Harriet Tubman it's called "Harriet Tubman-Lydia Laws Hall."

5) Delaware State University has a campus called "DSU ___."

6) Delaware State University's motto is Enter to Learn, Go Forth and ____.

Down

1) Delaware State University has an _____ Program that provides students with education and experience in preparation for careers in the aviation industry.

2) Delaware State University undergraduates are required to complete the General Education Program, which includes: seven core courses, twelve foundation courses (across the curriculum) and the Senior ____ Experience.

Directions: Read and answer the questions. These are your opinions so the answers will vary.

If you could meet a musician or group, who would it be?

What's your favorite thing to learn about in school?

In your free time, what do you like to do?

Directions: Unscramble the words below about DSU. See if you can get the bonus word.

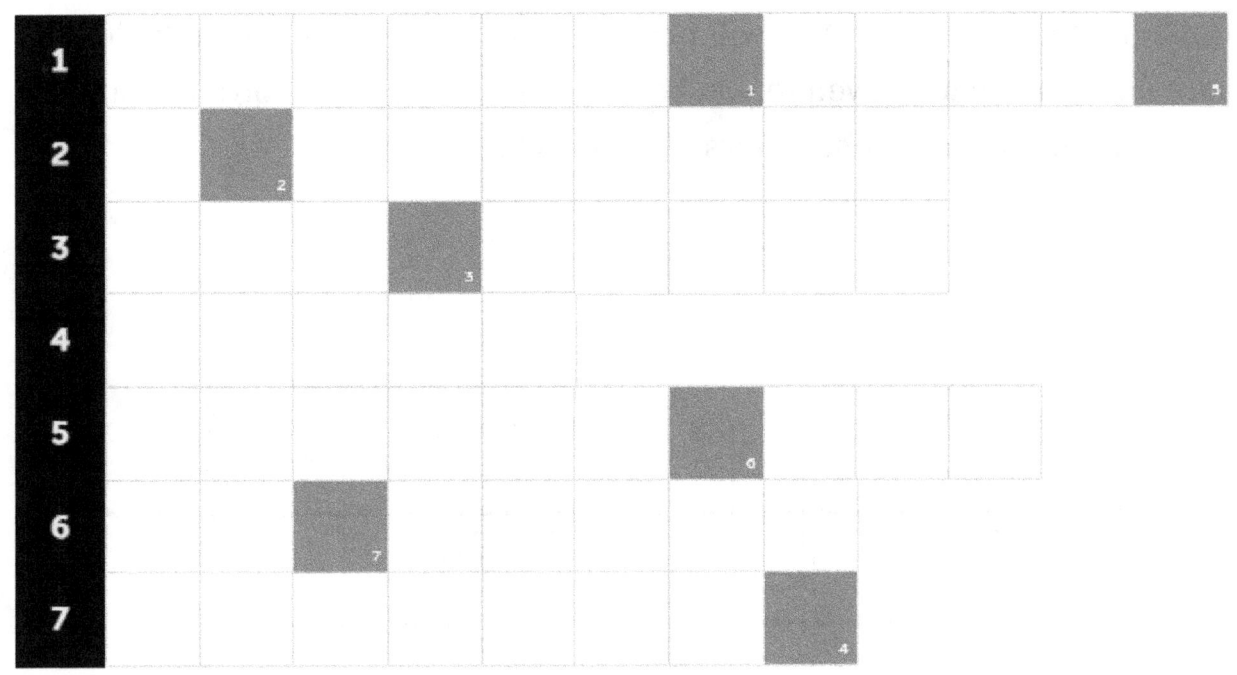

BONUS WORD

Unscramble Words

1) imgedhntiubl
2) tnlaenoyl
3) edrhycrre
4) drevo
5) iithmsaneu
6) isssbune
7) ationiav

Directions: This is the WGLT Challenge. Solve the cryptogram. As the puzzle solver, you need to find which number belongs to which character. And this can be pretty challenging! You will need to match the number with the letter. There are some letters given to you below. This will help you solve the other words and unlock more characters. **Good Luck.**

Solution:

THE WHOLE PURPOSE OF EDUCATION IS TO TURN MIRRORS INTO WINDOWS.

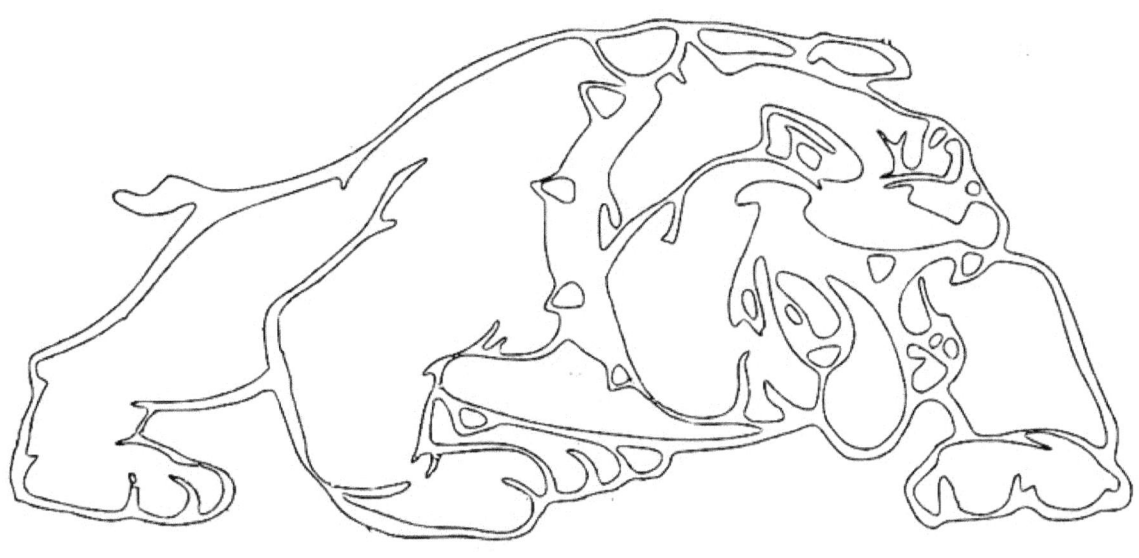

1869 – PRESENT

LEFT BLANK ON PURPOSE

Tougaloo College

Tougaloo College

Tougaloo College

Tougaloo College

Tougaloo College

Tougaloo College

Directions: read the bio below and answer the following questions.

Tougaloo College is a private HBCU that is dedicated to preparing its students to be lifelong learners who are committed to leadership and service in a global society through its diverse undergraduate and graduate programs. It was founded in 1869 in Jackson, MS, on one of the largest former plantations in central Mississippi. The Washington Hall contained classrooms and a lecture hall and Boarding Hall was a two-story building with a kitchen and dining hall, a laundry facility and dormitories for 30 female students. In 1873, Tougaloo College added a theological department for students who wanted to enter the Christian ministry and they expanded the school's industrial department by adding a cotton gin and an apparatus for grinding corn and by developing a facility for the manufacture of simple furniture on site. Tougaloo College is referred to as the "Cradle of the Civil Rights Movement in Mississippi" because of the significant role the college played in advancing the fundamental principles of equality, freedom, justice and America's promise.

1. Where was Tougaloo College founded at?
   A. Tougaloo, MS
   B. Jackson, MS
   C. Madison, MS
2. What year was Tougaloo College established?
   A. 1869
   B. 1861
   C. 1870
3. What is Tougaloo sometimes referred to as?
   A. Cradle of the graves in Mississippi
   B. Cradle of the Civil Rights Movement in Mississippi
   C. Cradle of humankind in Mississippi

Directions: Find the words associated with Tougaloo College.

B	Y	O	L	L	A	H	-	E	R	I	H	S	R	Y	A	D	M
H	R	T	O	U	G	A	L	O	O	-	N	I	N	E	U	A	E
G	I	K	C	Z	V	L	X	V	C	C	R	K	B	A	U	E	D
R	W	H	E	R	E	-	H	I	S	T	O	R	Y	O	R	A	G
A	W	I	E	F	Q	Y	Y	T	O	E	T	G	K	U	D	S	A
K	G	E	U	U	X	D	M	B	E	E	M	E	T	D	K	Q	R
L	U	E	L	C	L	R	Z	F	D	R	I	U	X	Q	T	N	E
X	F	B	K	X	V	B	F	P	T	J	F	N	Z	O	R	Q	V
T	G	O	M	H	T	T	-	V	F	-	T	C	M	Z	C	L	E
D	G	Z	T	G	K	L	E	L	E	A	B	E	A	S	I	O	R
L	X	I	U	H	E	A	U	H	A	L	M	R	L	Q	P	J	S
R	M	D	Q	U	L	O	T	L	Y	Y	X	D	W	R	D	V	-
O	E	S	C	L	Y	-	Y	T	N	J	O	N	N	N	A	T	M
K	B	R	S	O	S	S	D	D	Z	T	B	R	L	A	H	C	U
I	G	X	L	T	P	C	E	R	B	F	T	I	C	K	O	P	S
F	A	E	E	L	A	D	Y	-	B	U	L	L	D	O	G	S	E
H	I	E	J	P	B	E	A	C	Z	P	M	V	I	W	K	W	U
N	M	N	O	S	K	C	A	J	U	O	V	P	E	G	K	K	M

Find These Words

LADY-BULLDOGS
SCARLET
MEETS-THE-FUTURE
AYRSHIRE-HALL
TOUGALOO-NINE

ROYAL-BLUE
WHERE-HISTORY
JACKSON
MEDGAREVERS-MUSEUM

Directions: Read and answer the questions. These are your opinions so the answers will vary.

If you could meet a historical figure, who would it be?

What's your favorite extracurricular class?

What is your favorite thing to do over the weekends?

Directions: Unscramble the words below about Tougaloo College. See if you can get the bonus word.

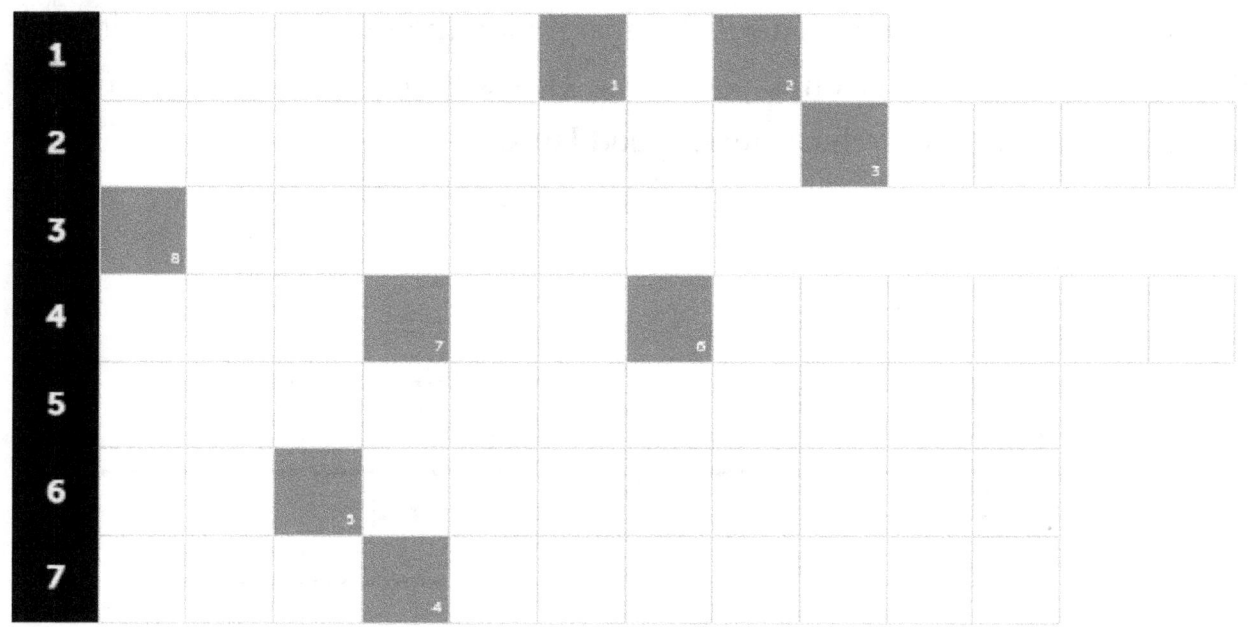

BONUS WORD

Unscramble Words

1) lalbuoyer
2) sarnltceerwma
3) saertlc
4) na-oeiluogotn
5) isisippssim
6) vardsrgeeme
7) cfelegdluon

Directions: This is the WGLT Challenge. Solve the cryptogram. As the puzzle solver, you need to find which number belongs to which character. And this can be pretty challenging! You will need to match the number with the letter. There are some letters given to you below. This will help you solve the other words and unlock more characters. **Good Luck.**

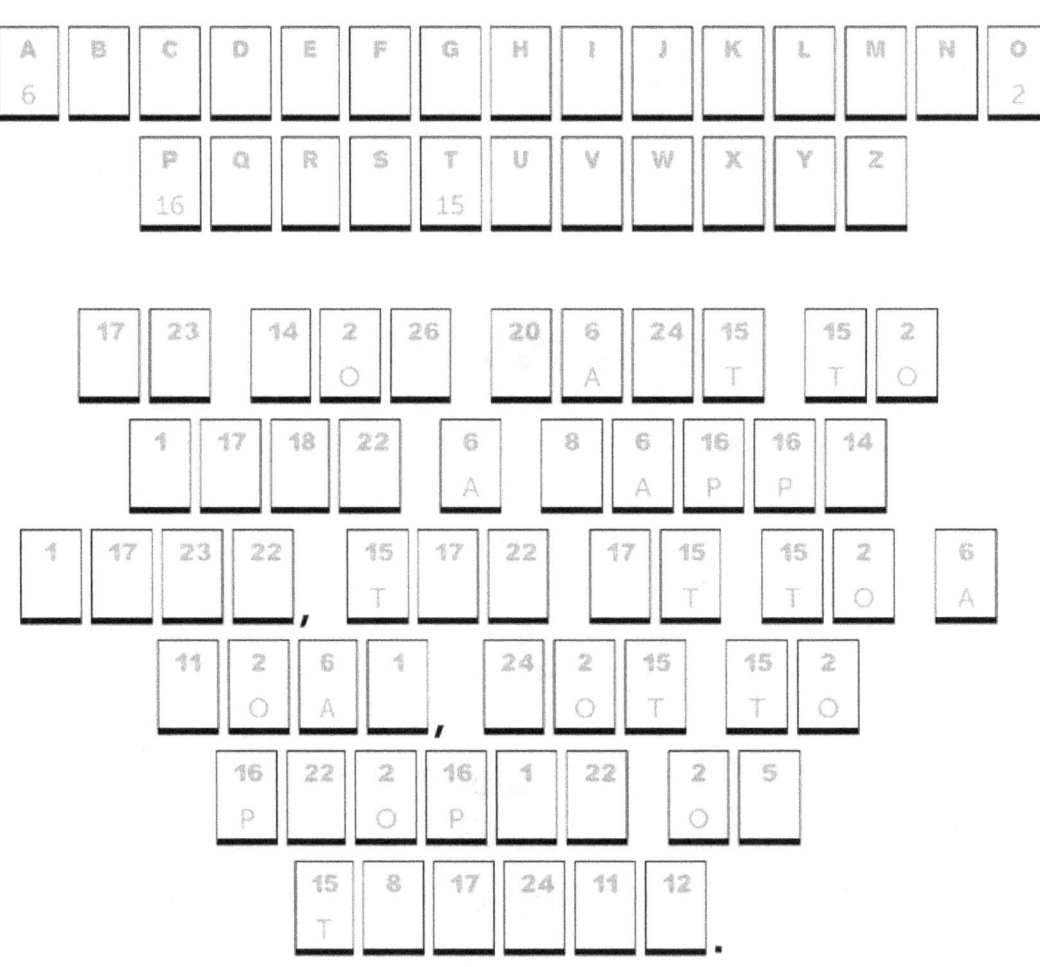

178

Morgan State

University

Morgan State

University

1867 – PRESENT

LEFT BLANK ON PURPOSE

Morgan State

University

Morgan State

University

Directions: read the bio below and answer the following questions.

Centenary Biblical Institute, which is now called Morgan State University (Morgan State or MSU), is a public research HBCU that is dedicated to the community, region, state, nation and world as an intellectual and creative resource by supporting, empowering and preparing high-quality, diverse graduates to lead the world. It was founded in 1867 in Baltimore, MD, by the Baltimore Conference of the Methodist Episcopal Church The institution wanted to train young men in the ministry. In 1890, the institute was renamed Morgan College in honor of Rev. Lyttleton Morgan, who donated land to the college. In 1937, Morgan College became Morgan State College so that Maryland could provide more educational opportunities to its Black citizens since higher education was still segregated. In 1975, Morgan State added several doctoral programs and became Morgan State University.

1. Where did the name for Morgan College come from?
   A. The State Assembly of Maryland
   B. Baltimore Conference of Methodist Episcopal Church
   C. In honor of the Reverend Lyttleton Morgan
2. What year did Morgan College become an University?
   A. 1937
   B. 1890
   C. 1975
3. What type of college did MSU start as?
   A. Research school
   B. Ministry school
   C. Medical school

Directions: Answer the questions, to solve the crossword puzzle. You can use the internet if you get stuck on any question.

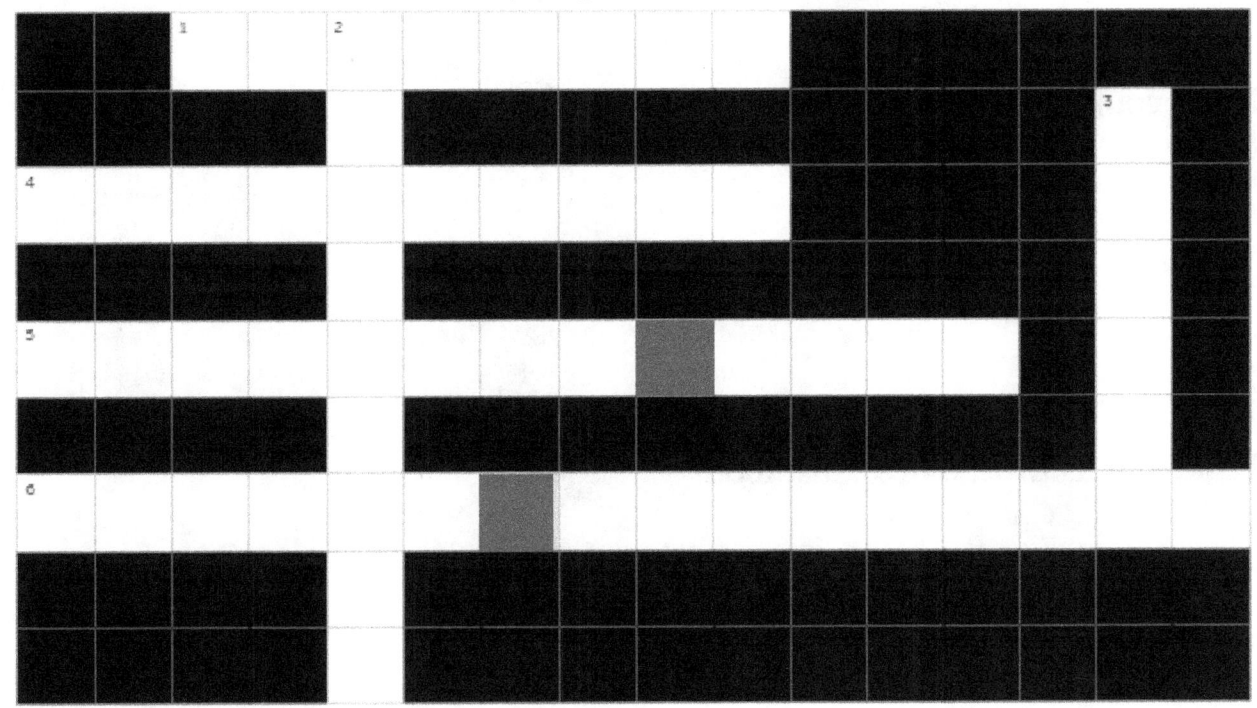

Across

1) Morgan State University was the only—historically black university to field a ____ team until the turn of the 20th century.
4) Morgan State University has the School of Global _____ and Communication.
5) Morgan State University's ____, was the oldest original building on the present Morgan campus in 1918.
6) Morgan State University has one of the nation's most prestigious university _____.

Down

2) Morgan State University was a ____ Biblical Institute in the beginning.
3) Morgan State University's motto is Growing the ____, Leading the World.

Directions: Read and answer the questions. These are your opinions so the answers will vary.

If you could go back to any period in time, which would you choose?

What's your favorite breakfast food?

What is a unique talent you have?

Directions: Unscramble the words below about MSU. See if you can get the bonus word.

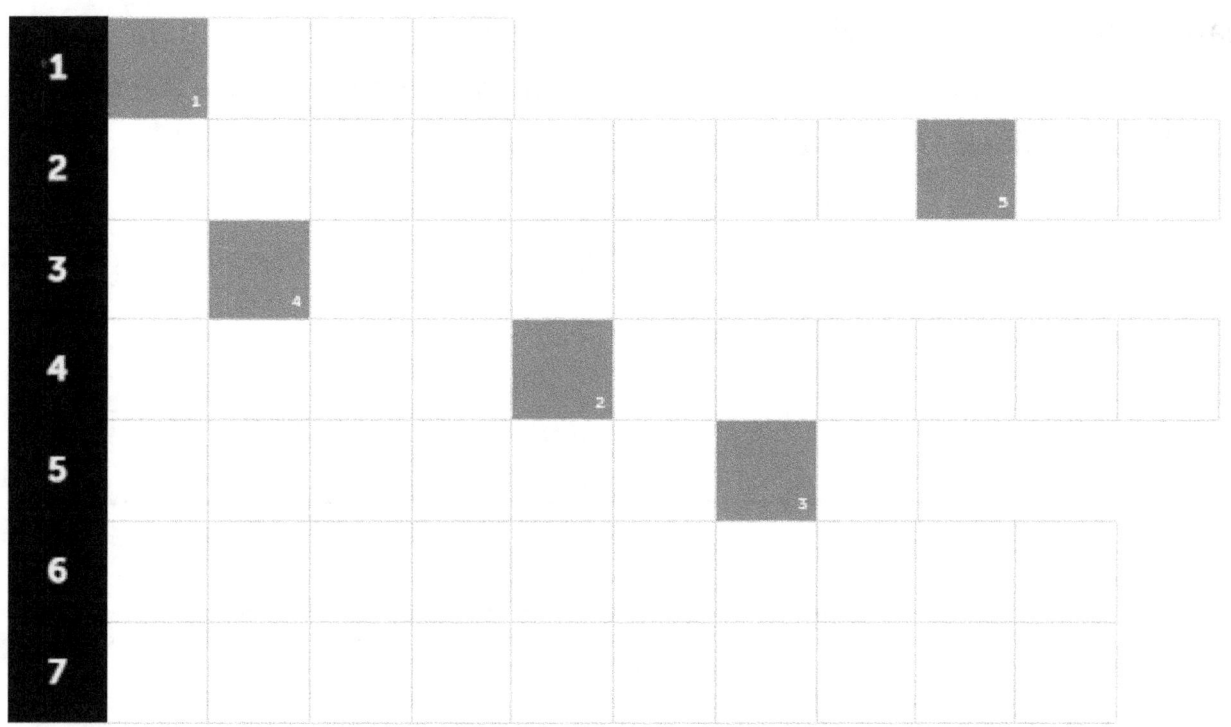

BONUS WORD

Unscramble Words

1) lube
2) dodiliwsnva
3) rgoean
4) eedoulngfcl
5) raoolcdt
6) tsgnapecra
7) orwicasokl

Directions: This is the WGLT Challenge. Solve the cryptogram. As the puzzle solver, you need to find which number belongs to which character. And this can be pretty challenging! You will need to match the number with the letter. There are some letters given to you below. This will help you solve the other words and unlock more characters. **Good Luck.**

1869 – PRESENT

LEFT BLANK ON PURPOSE

Dillard University

Dillard University

Dillard University

Dillard University

Dillard University

Dillard University

Directions: read the bio below and answer the following questions.

Straight University, which is now Dillard University, is a private HBCU that is dedicated to producing graduates who excel, become world leaders and are broadly educated, culturally aware and concerned with improving the human condition. It was founded in 1869 in New Orleans, LA, in response to the post-Civil War need to educate newly freed African Americans. In 1873, New Orleans University was established to fill the demand for the education of African Americans. In 1915, Straight University was renamed Straight College to better reflect the limitations of its curriculum. In 1934, New Orleans University merged with Straight College to form Dillard University. It was named after James H. Dillard. The university offers a traditional liberal arts curriculum rather than non-professional vocational training and maintains close engagement with the Black community through "various education extension programs, societies and clubs."

1. Which colleges merged to create Dillard University?
   A. Straight College
   B. New Orleans University
   C. University of Louisiana at Lafayette
2. What year did Dillard become an University?
   A. 1873
   B. 1934
   C. 1915
3. How did Dillard University get it's name?
   A. James H. Dillard
   B. United Church of Christ
   C. United Methodist Church

Directions: Find the words associated with Dillard University.

```
V H O W A R D - H O U S E J A V T I
Z V H B J L G L I J S Q O Y V H M G
I R O Y A L - B L U E & W H I T E E
M I O J N E L T K T B J V R J P G D
Z X N A Z S O U S W O P K A A X V C
R Q X B U M U I A M H W U Y H E V I
Z Z B L G H I Z D U N W K - Y Q X V
U B M E Z O S D Z Q H Y I C I O T I
K X F N Z K I U R S Q A X H J L J L
H U L P S Z A M D B F O U A W A A -
O E Y J X O N U E V A A B R M K V R
V R C F M U A L N Z B Z C L R J K I
X N E P U V E Z S W K T F E X M Z G
D U A L - D E G R E E M E S D T P H
I N S T I T U R E - O F - J A Z Z T
S E Y M O U R - S T R A I G H T I S
D B L E U - D E V I L S P N D U X L
Y T G C Q B O P U U M G K T N E X E
```

Find These Words

INSTITURE-OF-JAZZ BLEU-DEVILS
ROYAL-BLUE&WHITE LOUISIANA
RAY-CHARLES DUAL-DEGREE
HOWARD-HOUSE SEYMOUR-STRAIGHT
CIVIL-RIGHTS

Directions: Read and answer the questions. These are your opinions so the answers will vary.

If you could meet a cartoon character in real life, who would you pick?

Who is a friend at school that you know you can count on?

What is one thing you want to know about your teacher?

Directions: Unscramble the words below about Dillard University. See if you can get the bonus word.

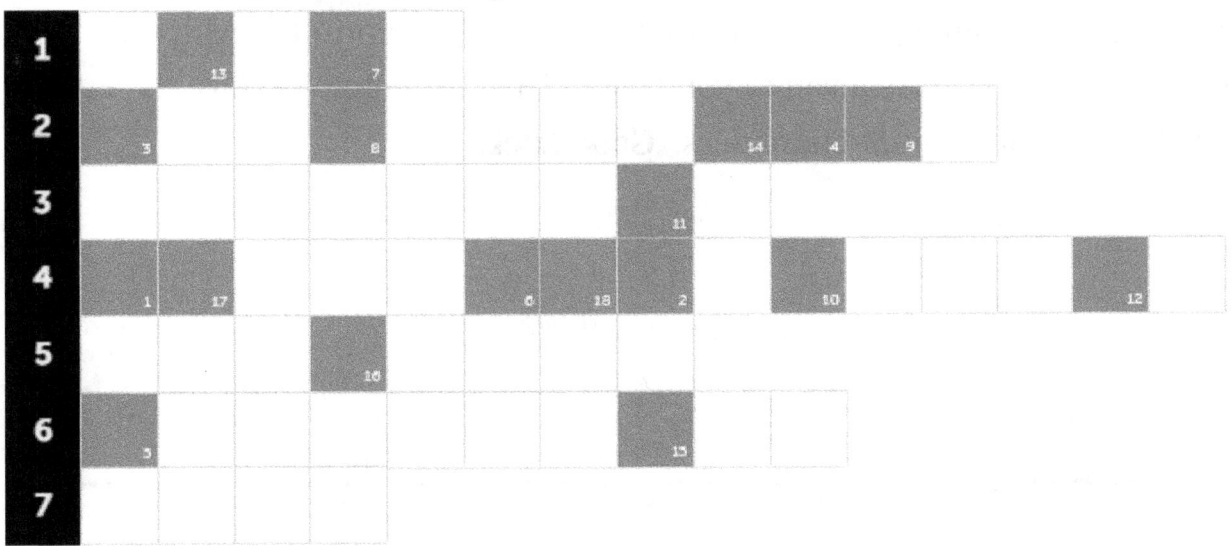

BONUS WORD

Unscramble Words

1) teiwh
2) hrloeflcroed
3) ralbluoey
4) liteecgtaholgsr
5) larciviw
6) ewnslroena
7) zjza

Directions: This is the WGLT Challenge. Solve the cryptogram. As the puzzle solver, you need to find which number belongs to which character. And this can be pretty challenging! You will need to match the number with the letter. There are some letters given to you below. This will help you solve the other words and unlock more characters. **Good Luck.**

North Carolina
Central University

North Carolina
Central University

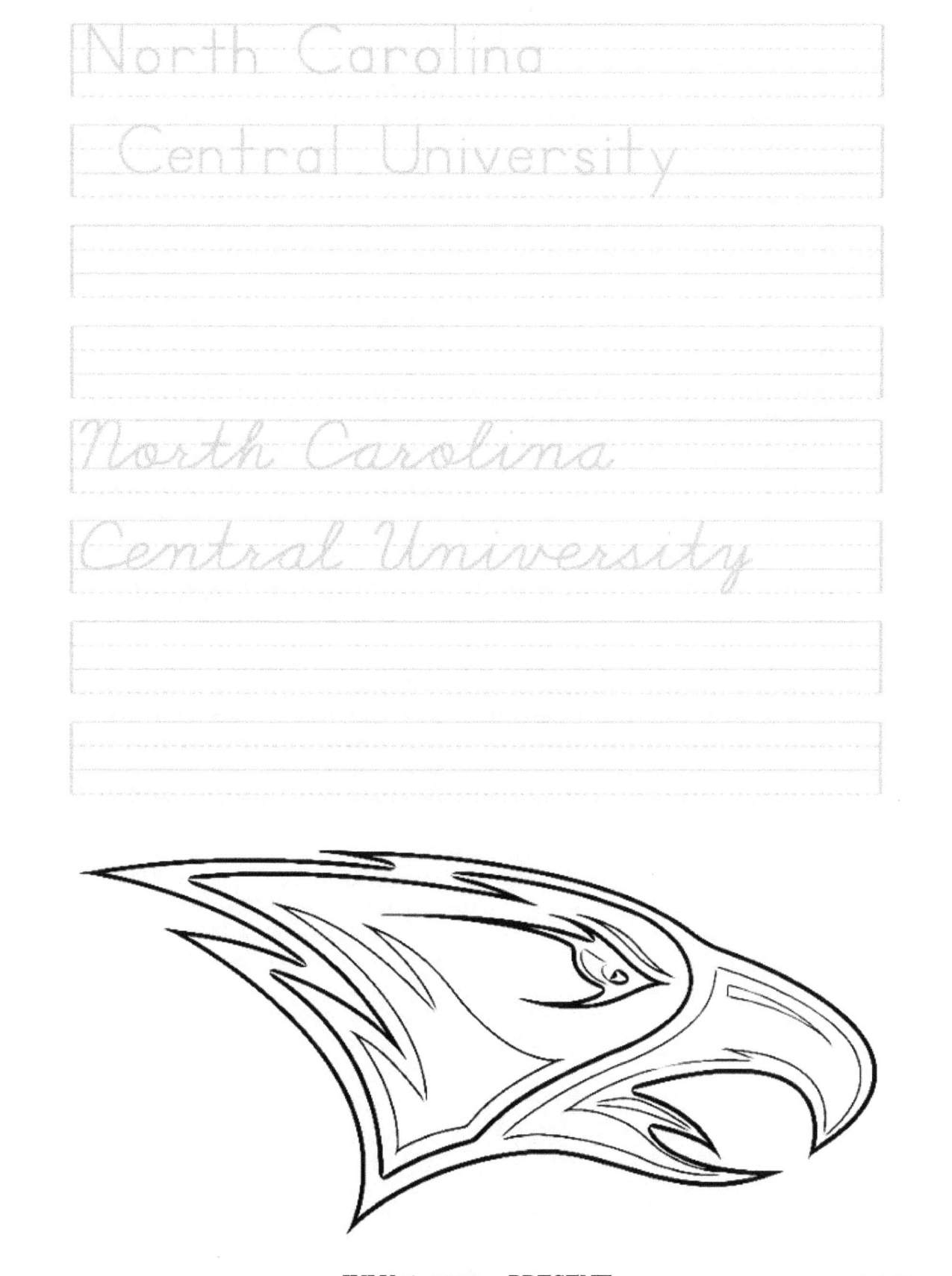

JULY 5, 1910 – PRESENT

LEFT BLANK ON PURPOSE

North Carolina

Central University

North Carolina

Central University

Directions: Read the Bio below. Answer the questions that follow.

National Religious Training School and Chautauqua for the Colored Race, which is now called North Carolina Central University (NCCU or NC Central), is a public HBCU that is dedicated to preparing students to become global leaders and practitioners who transform communities. It was founded on July 5, 1910, in Durham, NC, in the Hayti District by Dr. James E. Shepard. The institution was sold and reorganized in 1915 as the National Training School. In 1923, the state started funding the institution, so it was renamed Durham State Normal School for Negroes. In 1925, by expanding the programs to a four-year curriculum with a variety of majors, the General Assembly converted the institution into the North Carolina College for Negroes. In 1947, graduate courses were added, so the General Assembly changed the name of the institution to North Carolina College at Durham (NCCD). In 1969, the college became one of the state's regional universities and the name was changed to North Carolina Central University.

1. Who founded NC Central?
    A. Dr. James E. Shepard
    B. Margaret Olivia Slocum Sage
    C. American Missionary Association
2. What year did NCCU become an University?
    A. 1947
    B. 1969
    C. 1925
3. Why did our name get changed to NCCD ?
    A. They added a four-year curriculum
    B. They added graduate courses
    C. They got state funding

Directions: Answer the questions, to solve the crossword puzzle. You can use the internet if you get stuck on any question.

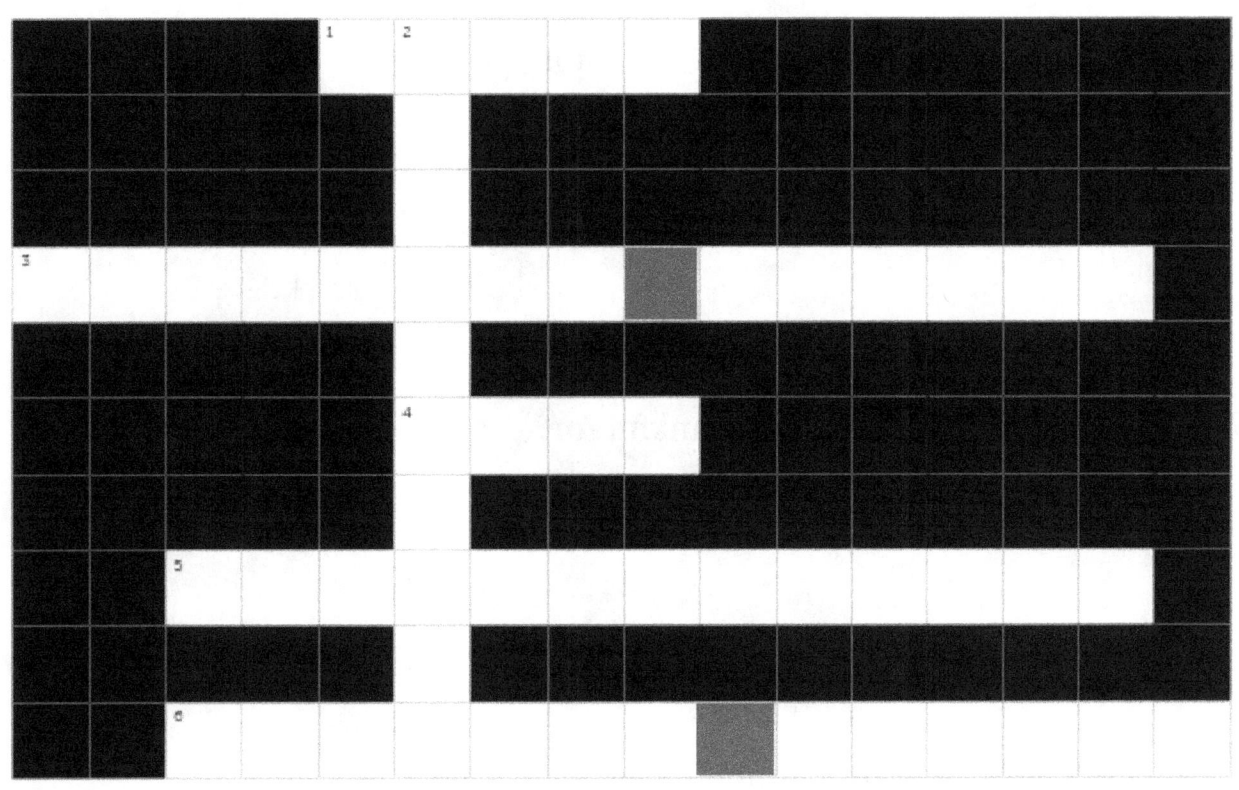

Across

1) NCCU nickname was given ____ by it's founder because Eagle's soar alone.

3) NCCU is listed on the National Register of _____.

4) NCCU is only about three miles east of ____ University.

5) NCCU is the home to The Julius L. Chambers Biomedical _____ Research Institute.

6) _____ contributed some private support for the school's founding for NCCU.

Down

2) NCCU was ____ by the Southern Association of Colleges and Secondary Schools as an "A" class institution in 1937.

Directions: Read and answer the questions. These are your opinions so the answers will vary.

If you could meet one celebrity, who would it be?

What is something that you are thankful for?

What is a family tradition that you have?

Directions: Unscramble the words below about NCCU. See if you can get the bonus word.

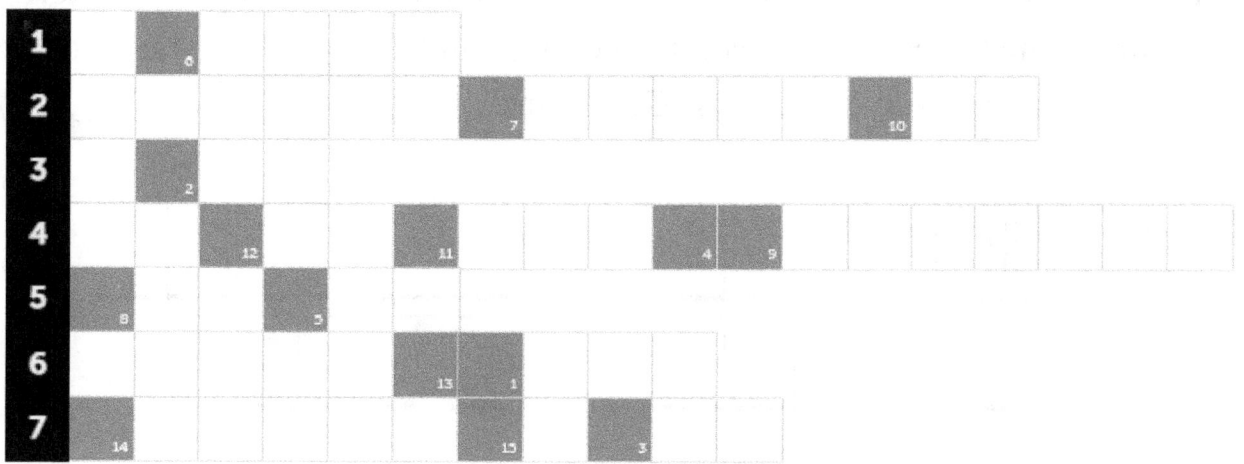

BONUS WORD

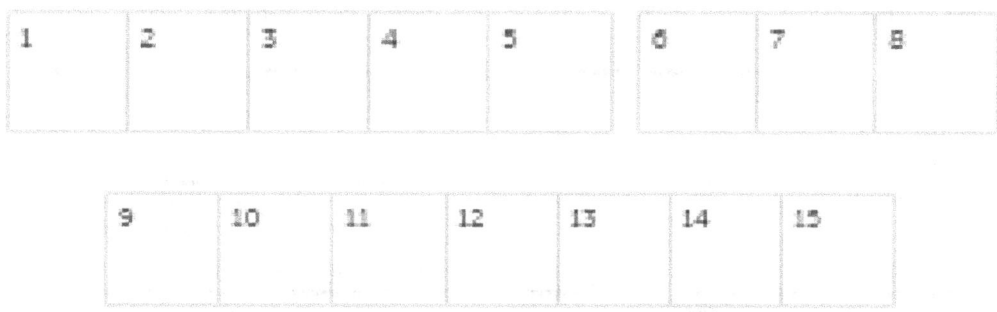

Unscramble Words

1) arnoom
2) oklsenyeanjnioh
3) aygr
4) teahevisllgriir-dc
5) dhramu
6) shntieiaum
7) leduegfncol

Directions: This is the WGLT Challenge. Solve the cryptogram. As the puzzle solver, you need to find which number belongs to which character. And this can be pretty challenging! You will need to match the number with the letter. There are some letters given to you below. This will help you solve the other words and unlock more characters. **Good Luck.**

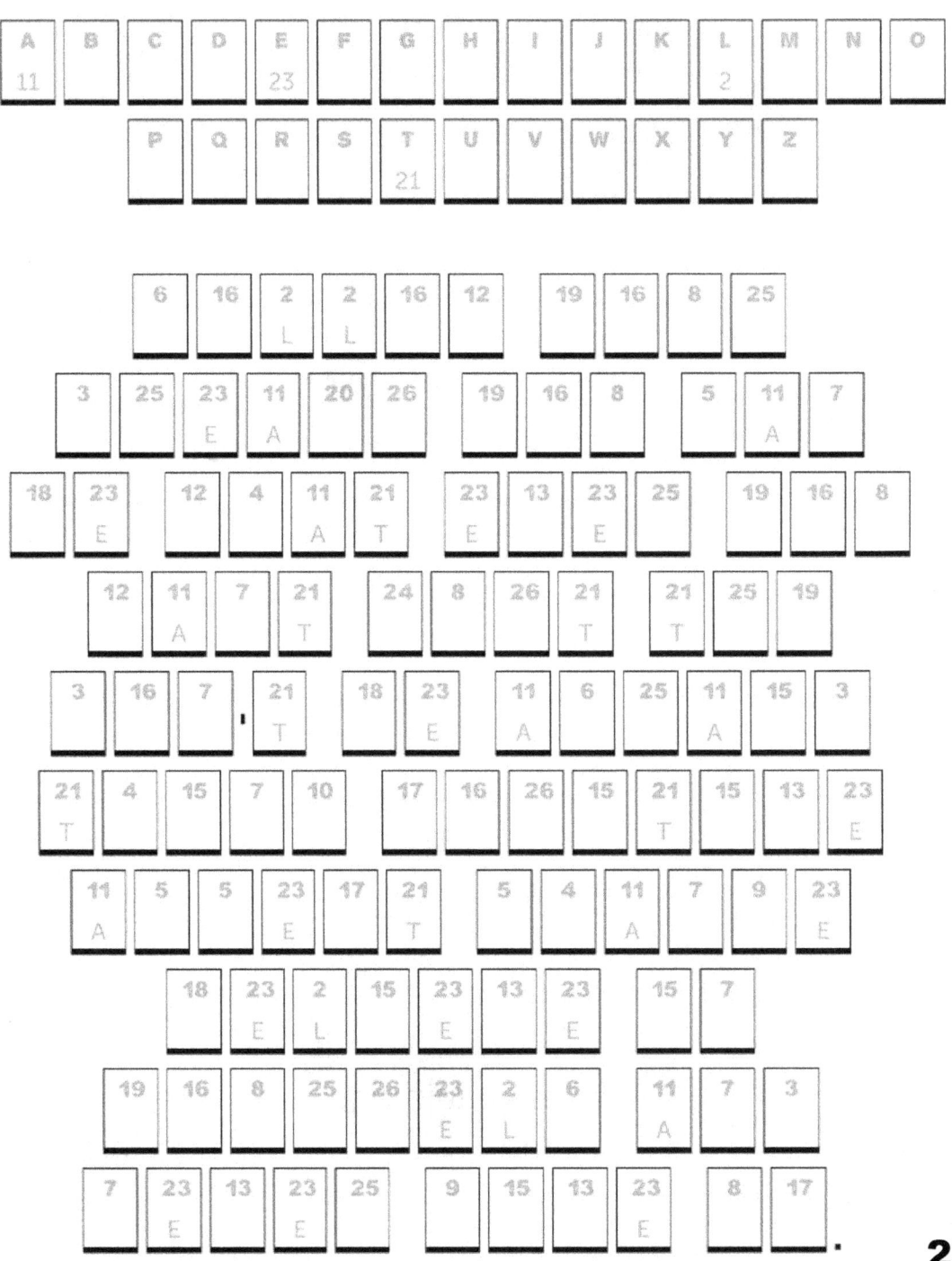

202

1. Where was Spelman founded at?
   A. Worcester, MA
   B. Atlanta, GA
   C. Richford, NY
2. What was our name prior to 1884?
   A. Spelman College
   B. Atlanta Baptist Female Seminary
   C. Spelman Seminary
3. Who is Spelman College named after?
   A. Harriet E. Giles's mother
   B. John D. Rockefeller's wife
   C. Sophia B. Packard's mother

Spelman College Answers

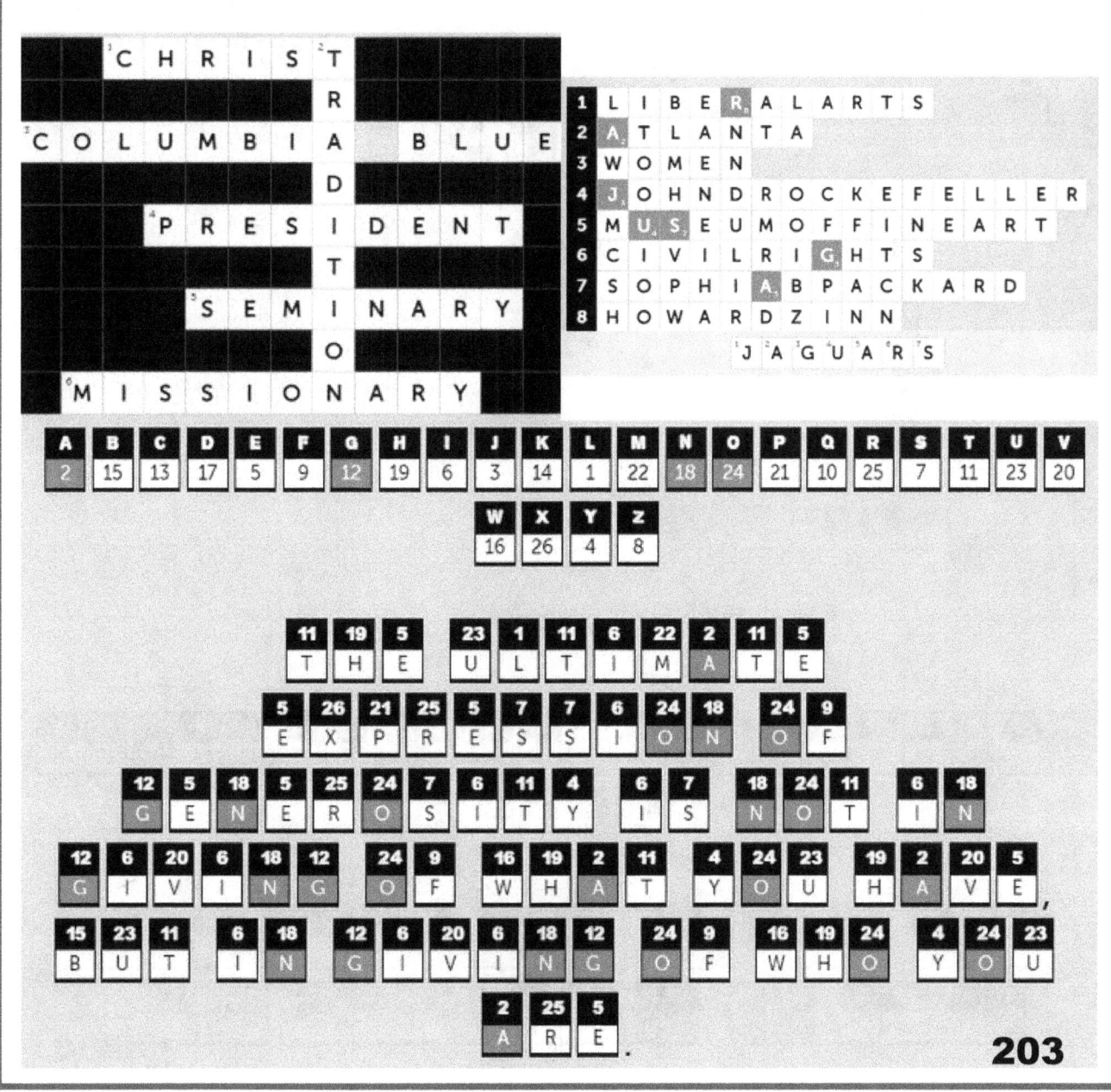

203

CSU Answers

1. **How did CSU come to be a college?**
   A. Wilberforce University created a new department
   B. AME created a new college
   C. State legislation was enacted
2. **What year did Wilberforce become a college?**
   A. 1947
   B. 1951
   C. 1941
3. **What is special about Wilberforce University?**
   A. It's the first college that was owned and operated by African-Americans
   B. They started Central State University
   C. They provide classical education

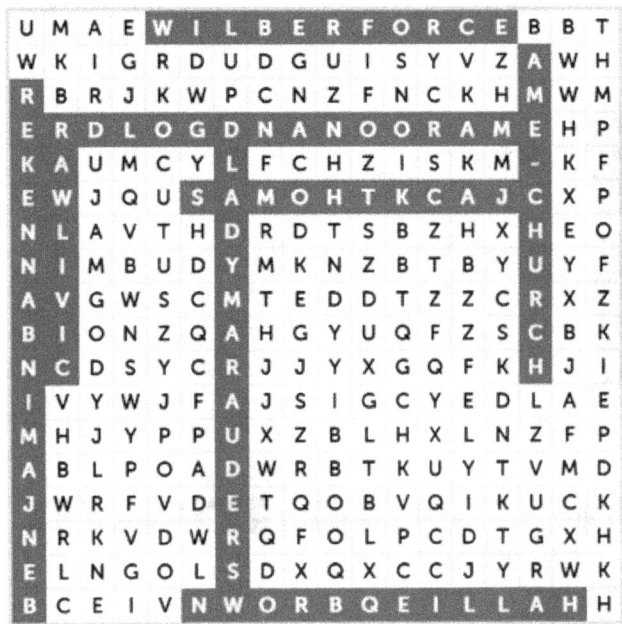

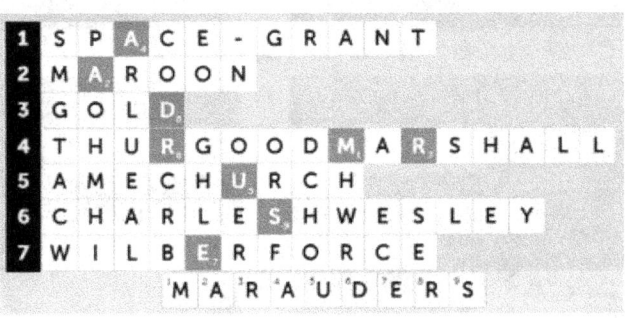

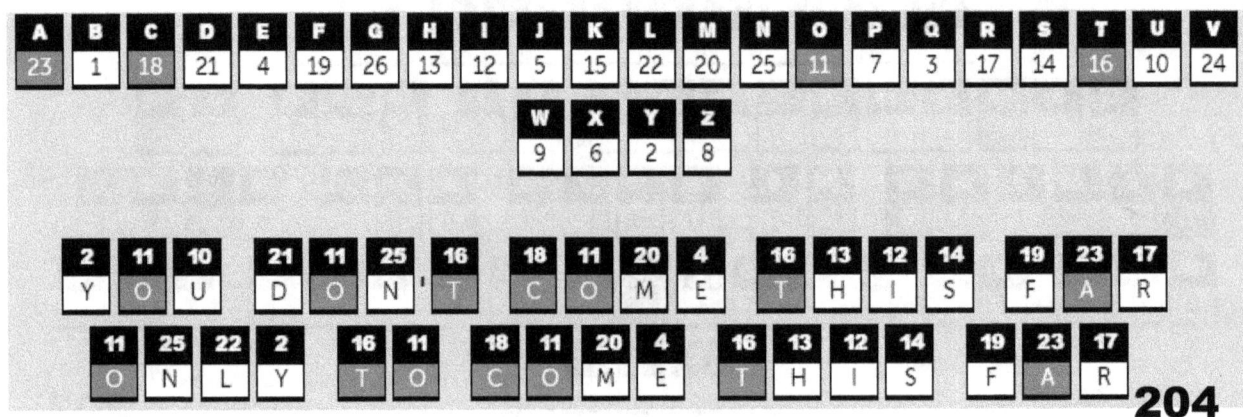

YOU DON'T COME THIS FAR
ONLY TO COME THIS FAR

Howard University Answers

1. What city was Howard founded in?
   A. Washington D.C.
   B. Atlanta, GA
   C. New York City, NY
2. Which sorority didn't get founded at Howard?
   A. Alpha Kappa Alpha
   B. Zeta Phi Beta
   C. Sigma Gamma Rho
3. What was HU first at doing at the University?
   A. first black medical school
   B. first black law school
   C. first black IT school

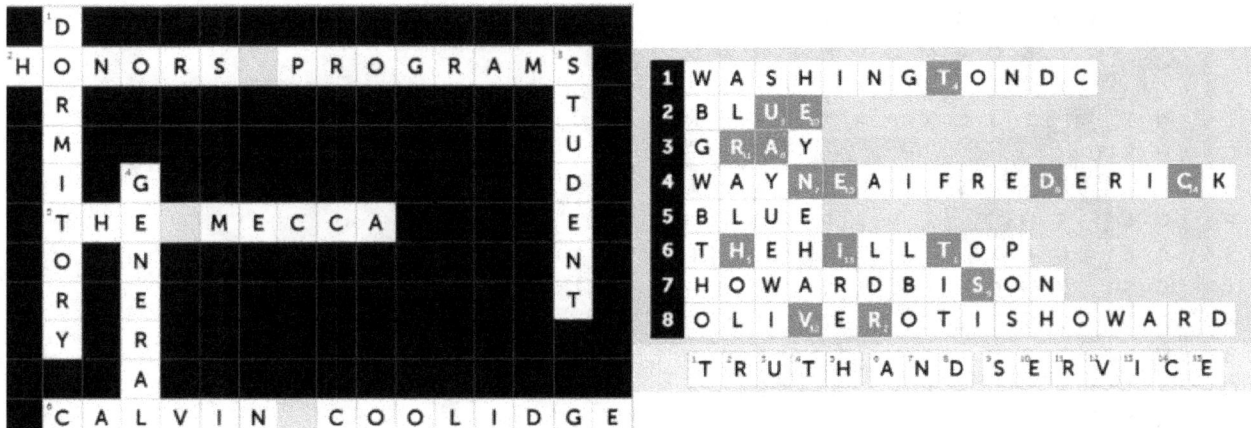

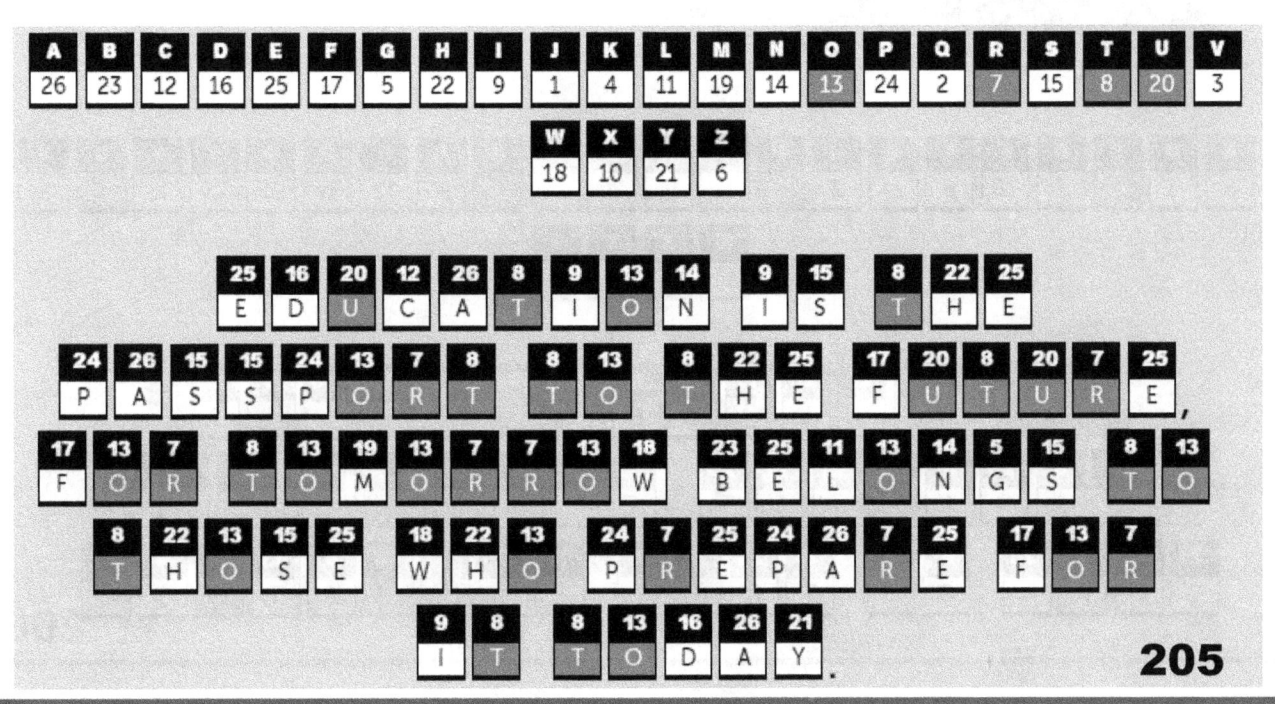

"EDUCATION IS THE PASSPORT TO THE FUTURE, FOR TOMORROW BELONGS TO THOSE WHO PREPARE FOR IT TODAY."

205

ASU Answers

1. Where was ASU founded at?
   A. Jackson, MS
   B. Lorman, MS
   C. The Bill Cosby show
2. What was Alcorn University the first in the U.S. for?
   A. First HBCU
   B. First land grant college
   C. First all male college
3. What was on the ASU land before we were founded?
   A. A farm
   B. A jail house
   C. A college

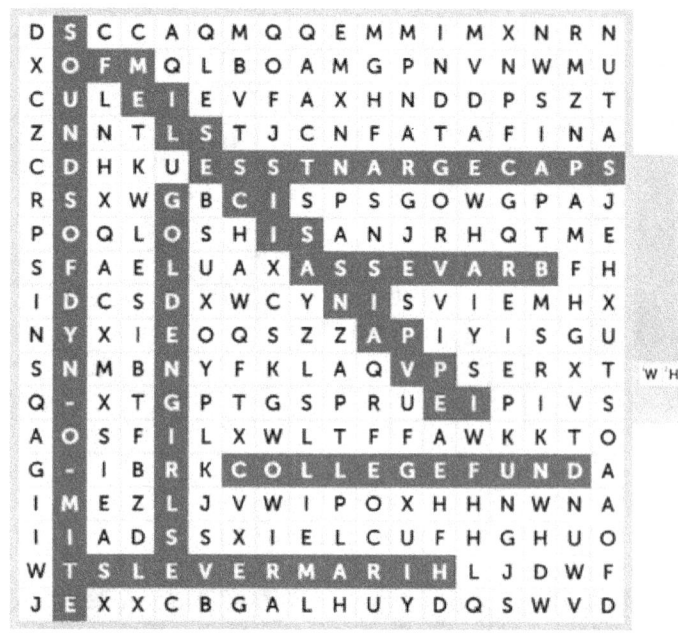

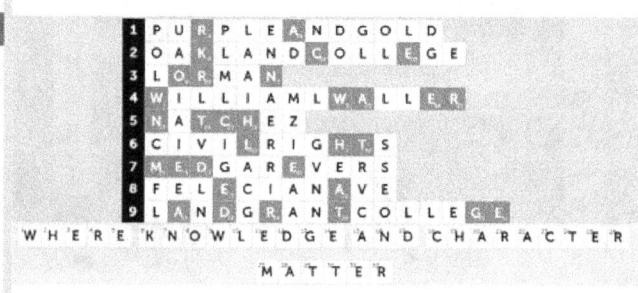

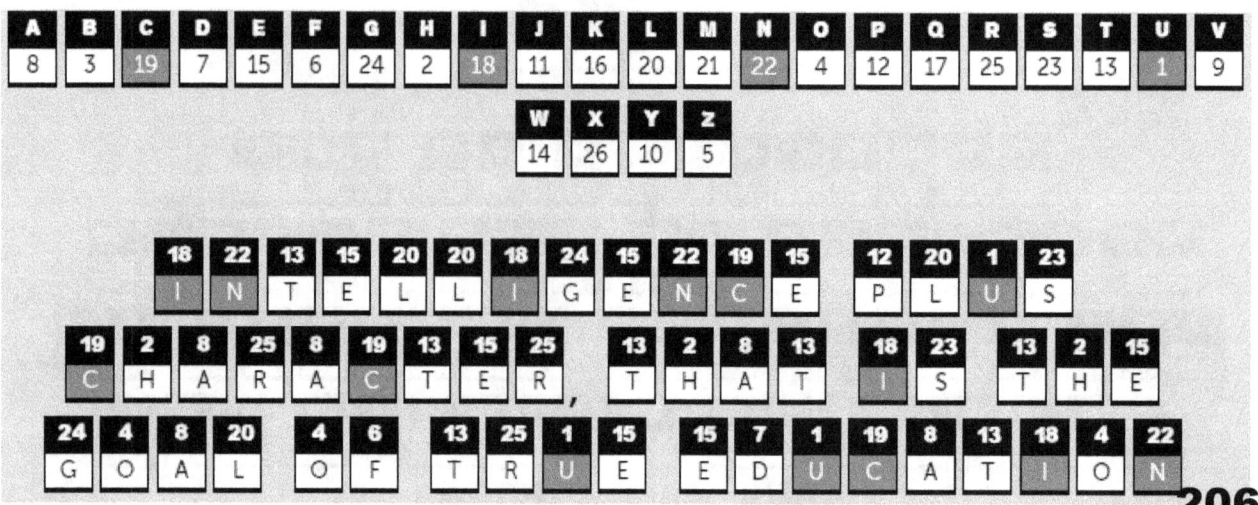

INTELLIGENCE PLUS CHARACTER, THAT IS THE GOAL OF TRUE EDUCATION

1. What was the universities name at the start?
   A. Xavier University
   B. Xavier University Preparatory School
   C. Xavier University of Louisiana
2. What year did XULA establish a pharmacy school?
   A. 1927
   B. 1925
   C. 1915
3. XULA is the only _____ HBCU?
   A. All Woman
   B. All Male
   C. Catholic

XULA Answers

Crossword:
- 1 down: COLLEGES
- 2 down: MILITARY
- 3 down: HEATH
- 4 down: MEDICA
- 5 across: GOLD DIGGA
- 6 across: HEALTH

Word puzzle:
1. NEW ORLEANS
2. GOLD AND WHITE
3. KATHARINE DREXEL
4. CATHOLIC
5. SUPERIOR GENERAL
6. C REYNOLD VERRET
7. CARDINAL DOUGHERTY

GOLD NUGGETS

A	B	C	D	E	F	G	H	I	J	K	L	M	N	O	P	Q	R	S	T	U	V
24	13	1	19	8	26	7	3	22	20	2	10	23	12	17	4	16	21	18	14	11	5

W	X	Y	Z
6	15	25	9

THE FUNCTION OF EDUCATION IS TO TEACH ONE TO THINK INTENSIVELY AND TO THINK CRITICALLY.

207

ECSU Answers

1. **What was the colleges name in the beginning?**
   A. Elizabeth City State College
   B. Elizabeth City State Colored Normal School
   C. Elizabeth City State University

2. **What year did the college become an university?**
   A. 1963
   B. 1939
   C. 1969

3. **What was ECSU before becoming a 4 year college?**
   A. It's always been a 4 year college
   B. It was a 2 year college
   C. It was a teaching school

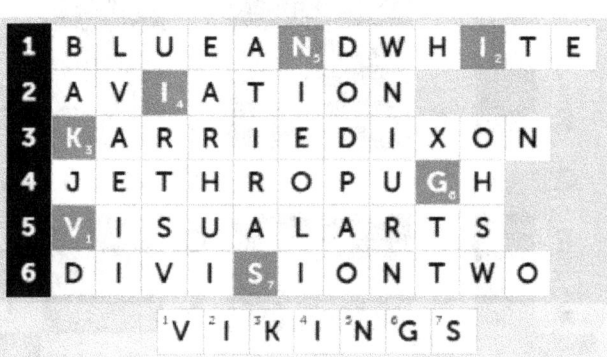

1. BLUE AND WHITE
2. AVIATION
3. KARRIE DIXON
4. JETHRO PUGH
5. VISUAL ARTS
6. DIVISION TWO

VIKINGS

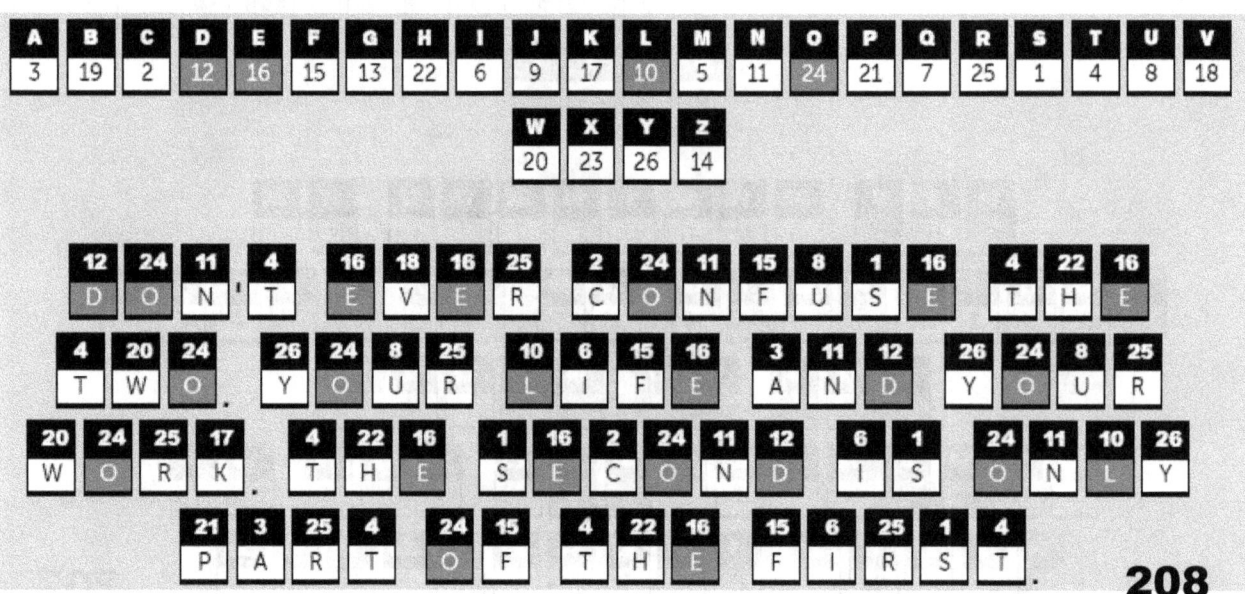

DON'T EVER CONFUSE THE TWO. YOUR LIFE AND YOUR WORK. THE SECOND IS ONLY PART OF THE FIRST.

208

HIU Answers

1. What national landmark is on HIU campus?
   A. Booker T. Washington National Monument
   B. Emancipation Oak
   C. The Mere Distinction of Colour
2. What year was HIU founded?
   A. 1863
   B. 1868
   C. 1870
3. What can you only find on HIU?
   A. Hampton University Museum
   B. Maggie Walker National Historic Site
   C. Black Soldiers Memorial

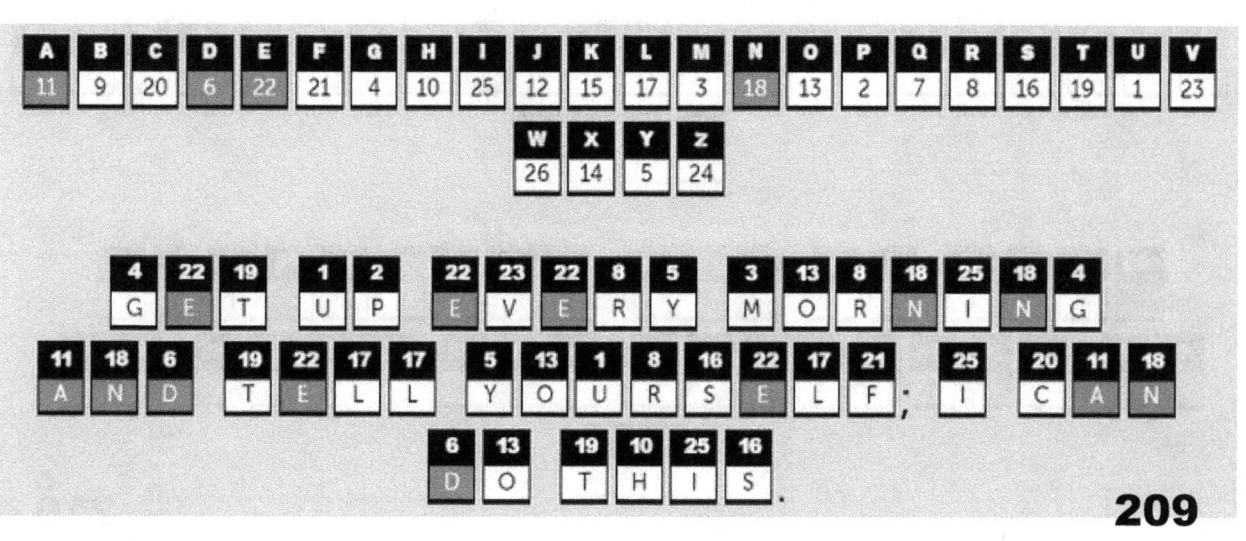

ASU Answers

1. Where was ASU located when it was founded?
   A. Montgomery, AL
   B. Mobile, AL
   C. Marion, AL
2. What year did I ASU move to Montgomery?
   A. 1867
   B. 1887
   C. 1928
3. What name did the University start out with?
   A. Lincoln Normal School of Marion
   B. Alabama State University
   C. Alabama State College

1. BLACK
2. MONTGOMERY
3. OLD GOLD
4. CONTRABAND OF WAR
5. QUINTON ROSS JR
6. BLACK BELT
7. HEALTH SCIENCES

HORNETS

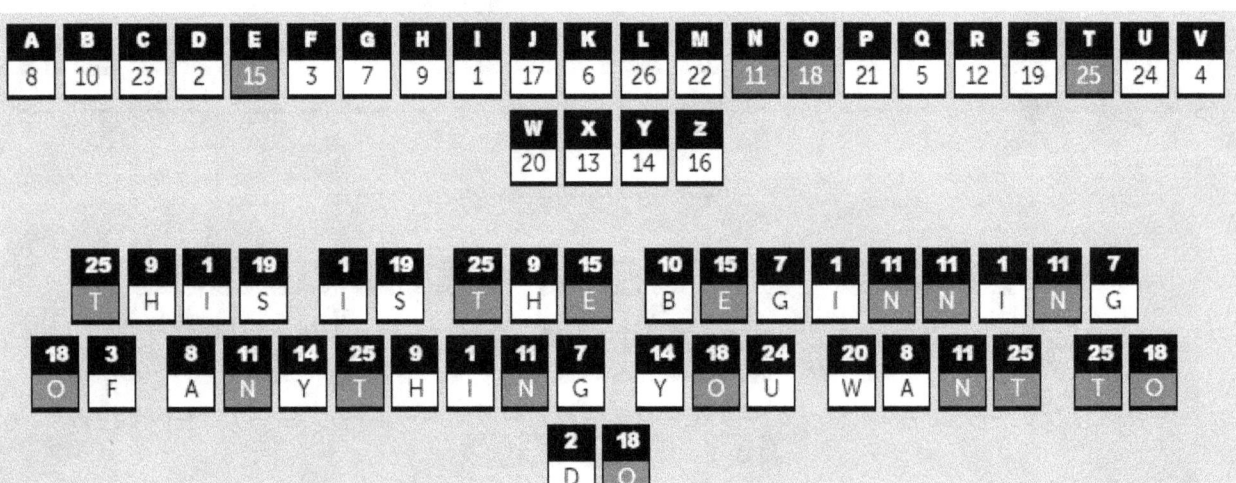

THIS IS THE BEGINNING OF ANYTHING YOU WANT TO DO.

1. Where was the college location when it was founded?
   A. Atlanta, GA
   B. Savannah, GA
   C. Augusta, GA
2. What year did we adopt the name Morehouse?
   A. 1897
   B. 1913
   C. 1887
3. Which is not a private all male college?
   A. Spelman College
   B. Wabash College
   C. Morehouse College

Morehouse College
Answers

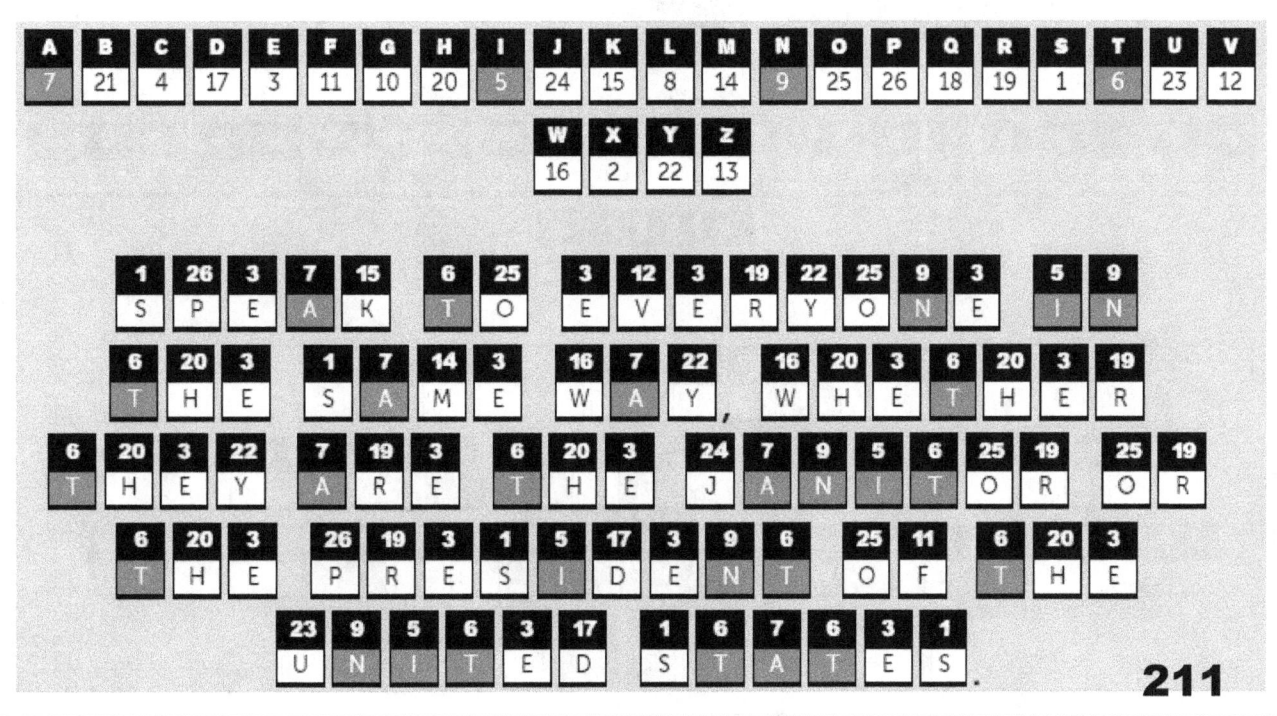

211

SUBR Answers

1. Which college isn't in the Southern University System?
   A. Southern University and A&M College
   B. Southern University
   C. Louisiana State University

2. What year was SUSLA established?
   A. 1904
   B. 1964
   C. 1956

3. There are __ college's in the Southern University System?
   A. 5
   B. 6
   C. 4

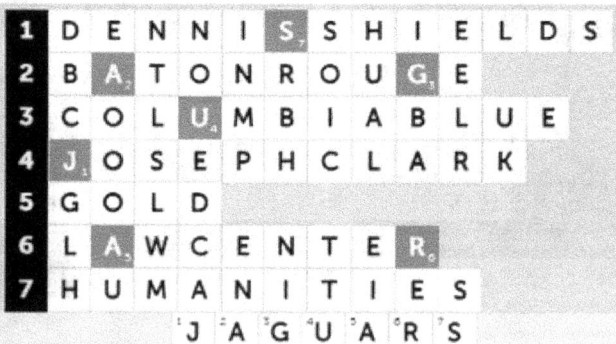

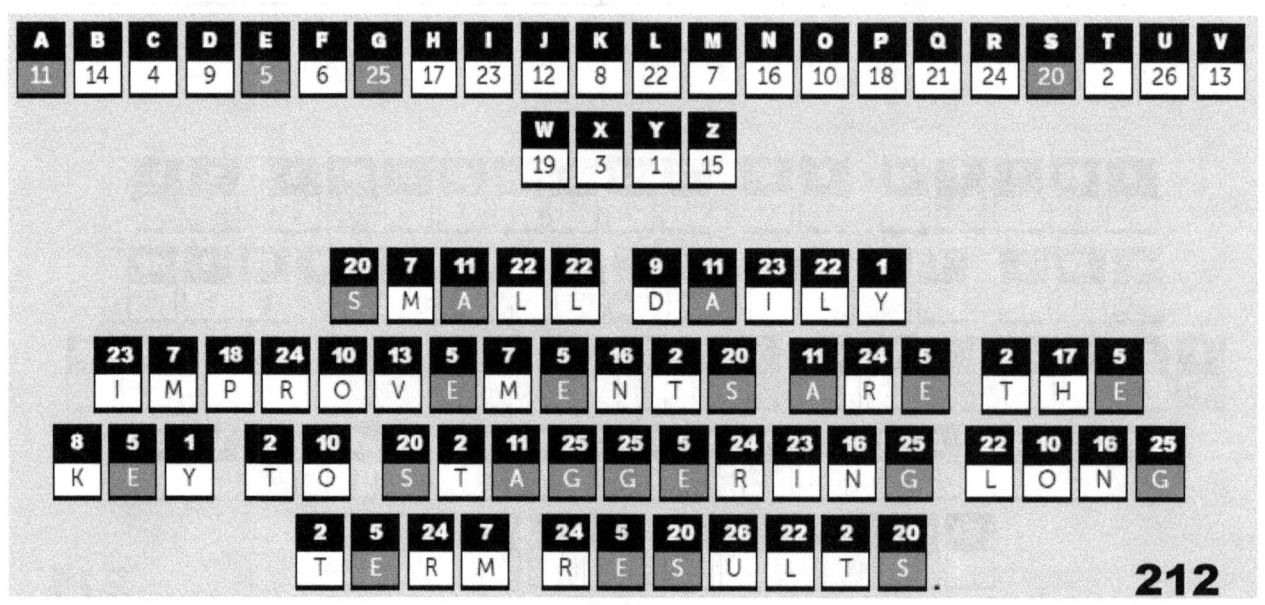

212

TU Answers

1. Which abbreviation is not a Tuskegee University?
   A. TSU
   B. Tuskegee
   C. TU
2. What year did we become a historic landmark?
   A. 1974
   B. 1966
   C. 1968
3. We are the only HBCU that is what?
   A. A Catholic College
   B. All Women College
   C. National Historic Site

Crossword (left):
- 1 Across: CRIMSON / PIPER / LAND
- Down: CYPHLI (CYPHILI...)
- PROFESSOR
- TRAINING PROGRAM
- CAMPUS DIGEST

Crossword (right):
1. CRIMSON AND OLD GOLD
2. CHARLOTTE MORRIS
3. SPACE GRANT
4. VETERINARY MEDICINE
5. TUSKEGEE AIRMEN
6. BOOKER T WASHINGTON
7. DAVID WILLISTON

KNOWLEDGE LEADERSHIP SERVICE

Cipher key:

A	B	C	D	E	F	G	H	I	J	K	L	M	N	O	P	Q	R	S	T	U	V
22	13	25	11	10	18	7	23	8	1	19	24	2	14	5	26	6	3	16	9	20	12

W	X	Y	Z
15	17	4	21

Decoded message:

THE PEOPLE WHO ARE CRAZY ENOUGH TO THINK THEY CAN CHANGE THE WORLD ARE THE ONES WHO DO.

213

NSU Answers

1. What event was going on when the college was founded?
   A. The Boulder (Hoover) Dam is completed.
   B. World War II
   C. The Great Depression
2. What year did NSU split from VSC?
   A. 1944
   B. 1969
   C. 1979
3. What name did I NSU start with?
   A. Virginia State College
   B. Norfolk Unit of Virginia Union University
   C. Norfolk State College

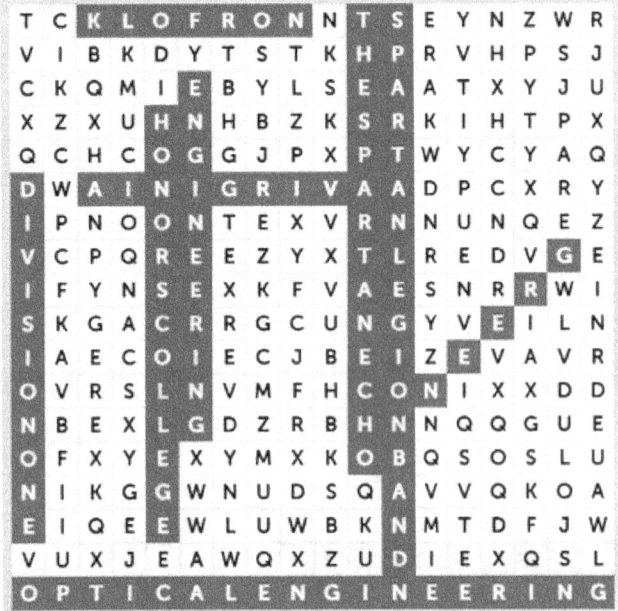

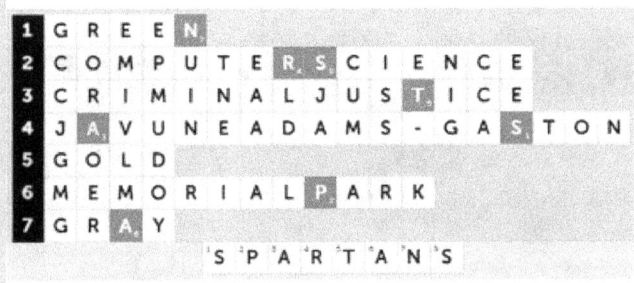

1. GREEN
2. COMPUTER SCIENCE
3. CRIMINAL JUSTICE
4. JAVUNE ADAMS-GASTON
5. GOLD
6. MEMORIAL PARK
7. GRAY

SPARTANS

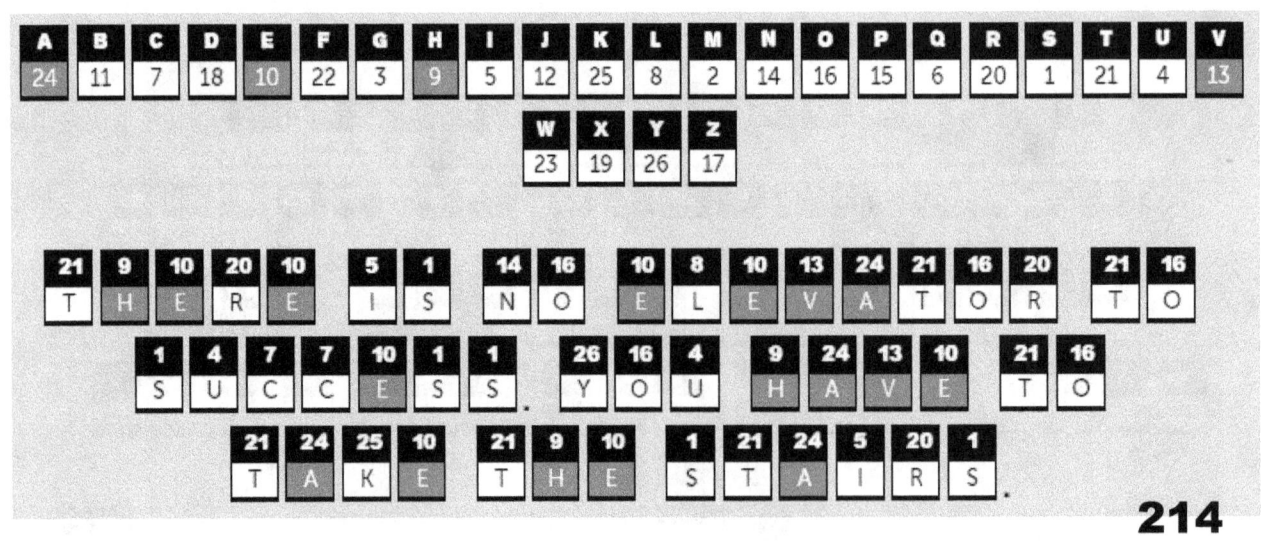

THERE IS NO ELEVATOR TO SUCCESS. YOU HAVE TO TAKE THE STAIRS.

214

FAMU Answers

1. This made FAMU an official institution of higher learning?
   A. The Second Morrill Act
   B. The 1905 Buckman Act
   C. The Servicemen's Readjustment Act (GI Bill)
2. What year did FAMU become an university?
   A. 1891
   B. 1953
   C. 1909
3. How many private HBCU's are in the state of Florida?
   A. One
   B. Three
   C. Two

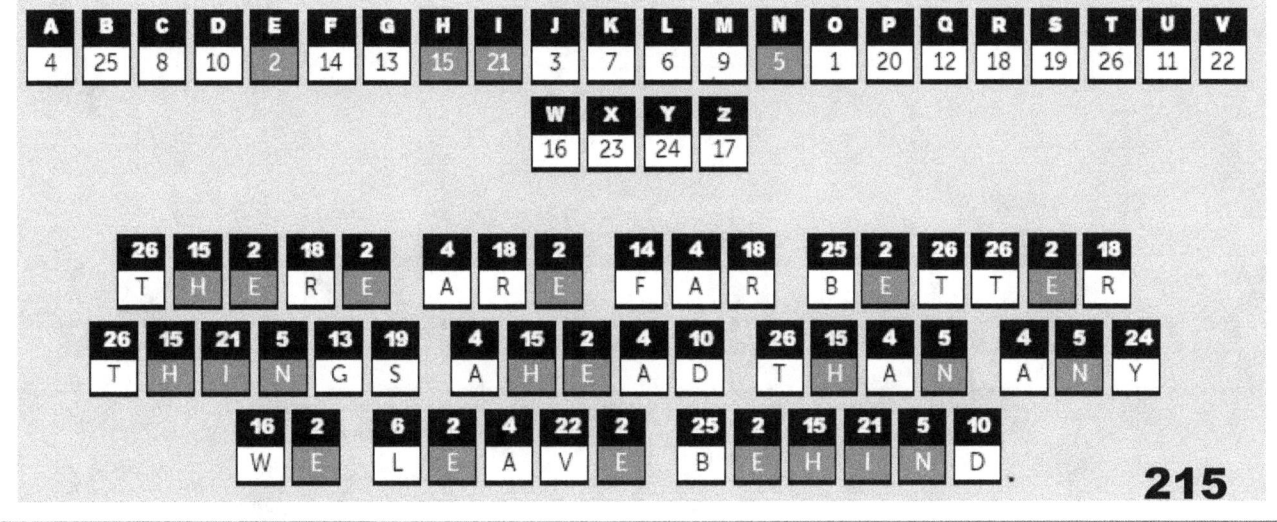

"THERE ARE FAR BETTER THINGS AHEAD THAN ANY WE LEAVE BEHIND."

215

JSU Answers

1. **What city did JSU start in?**
   A. Clinton, MS
   B. Jackson, MS
   C. Natchez, MS
2. **What year did Natchez Seminary become a college?**
   A. 1940
   B. 1944
   C. 1967
3. **Which acronym represents Jackson State University?**
   A. JSCC
   B. JSU
   C. JSS

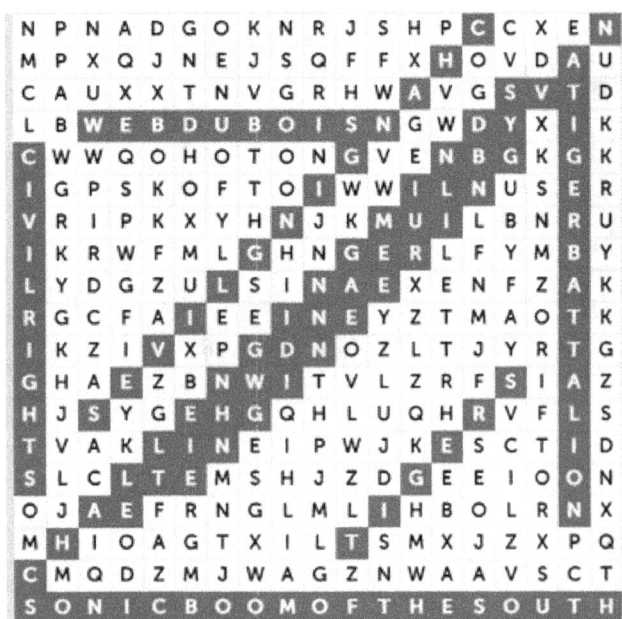

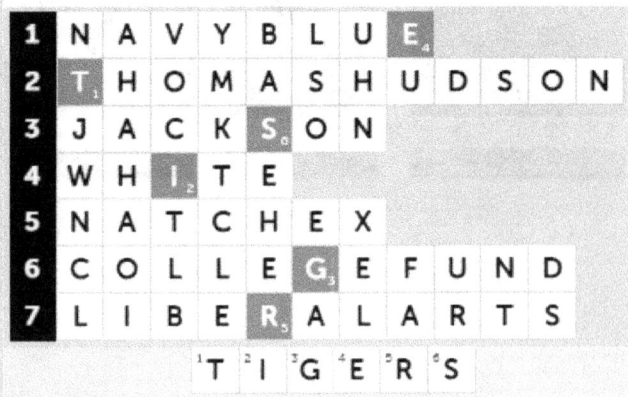

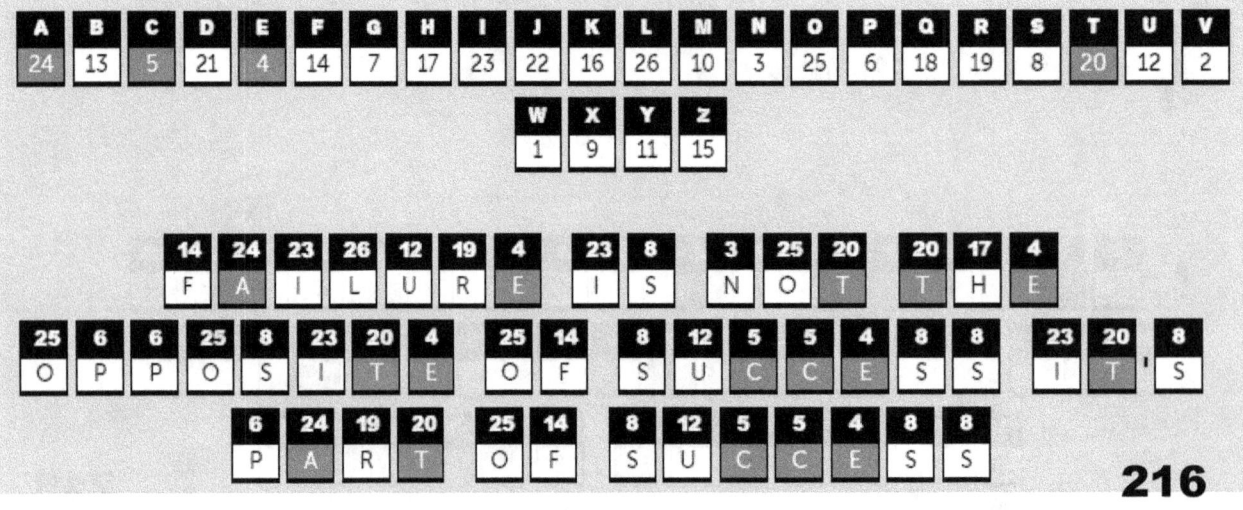

216

1. Which acronym is for North Carolina A&T ?
   A. UNC
   B. NCSU
   C. N.C. A&T
2. What year did A&T move to Greensboro, NC?
   A. 1892
   B. 1891
   C. 1893
3. What does A&T stand for in the college name?
   A. Agricultural and Technology
   B. Administrative and Technical
   C. Agricultural and Technical

N.C. AGT Answers

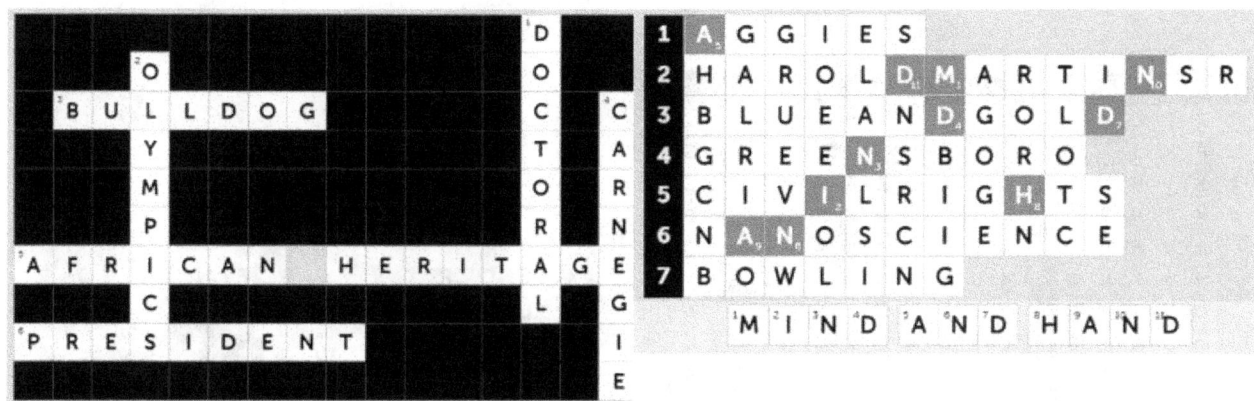

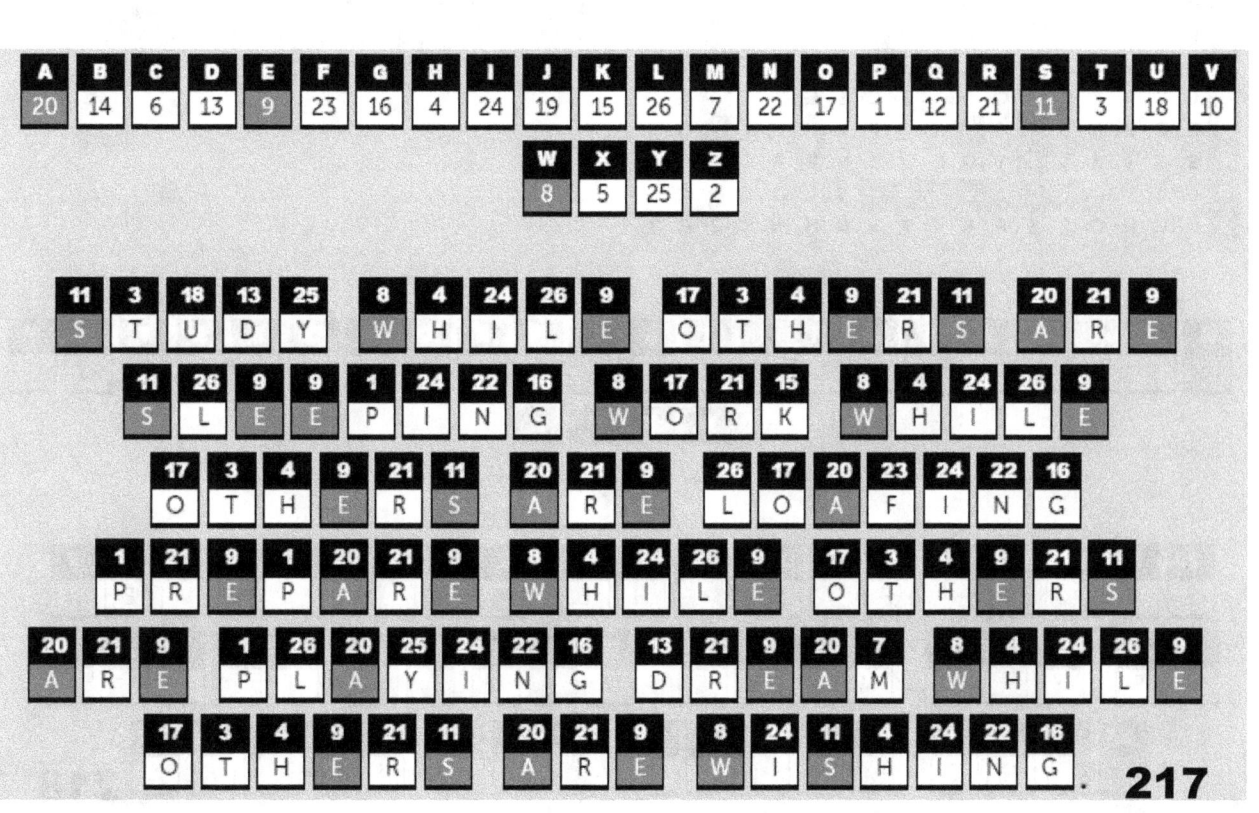

STUDY WHILE OTHERS ARE SLEEPING WORK WHILE OTHERS ARE LOAFING PREPARE WHILE OTHERS ARE PLAYING DREAM WHILE OTHERS ARE WISHING.

217

CAU
Answers

1. Which college was founded by the Methodist Church?
   A. Atlanta University
   B. Clark College
   C. Clark Atlanta Univeristy
2. What year did Atlanta and Clark merge together?
   A. 1929
   B. 1988
   C. 1869
3. What did Atlanta University do first in the South?
   A. Be the first HBCU
   B. Become an all male college
   C. Award a Bachelor's degree to African-American

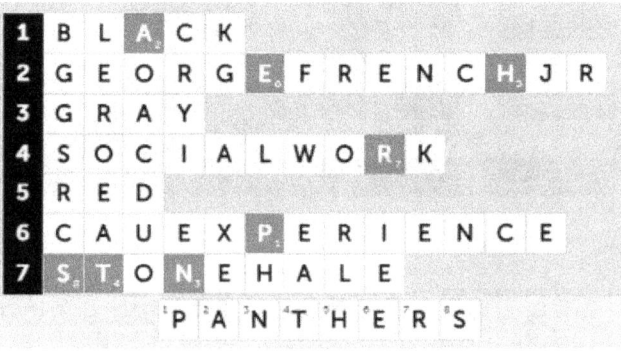

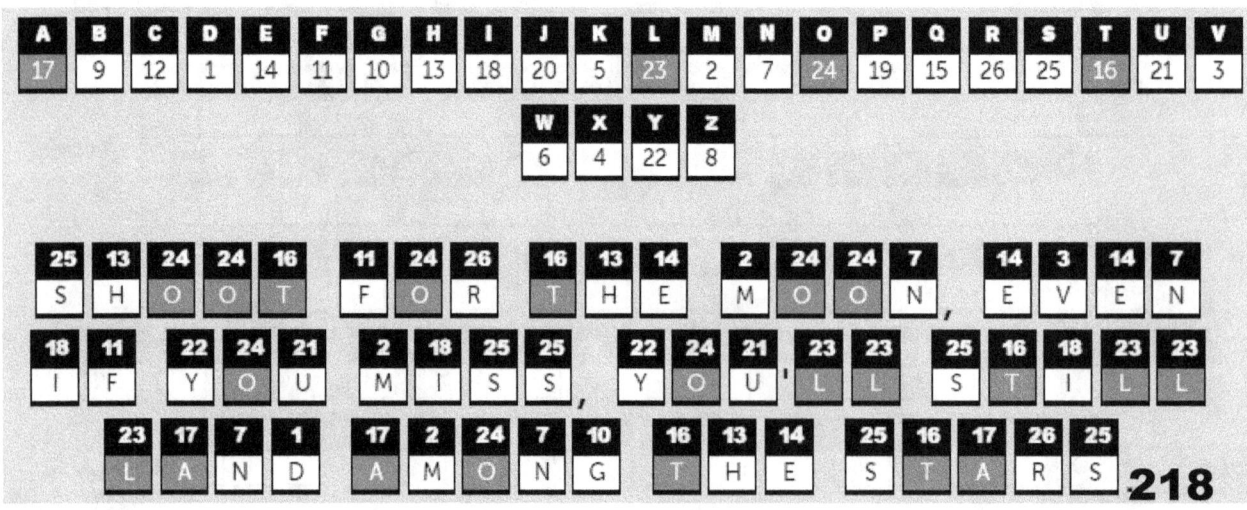

218

Fisk University Answers

1. What association is Fisk University apart of?
   A. South Florida Manufacturers Association
   B. State Societies in the Southeast
   C. Southern Association of Colleges and Schools
2. What rank was Clinton Fisk?
   A. Colonel
   B. General
   C. Major
3. Fisk is the ___ higher education institution in Nashville?
   A. Oldest University
   B. Oldest HBCU
   C. Oldest College

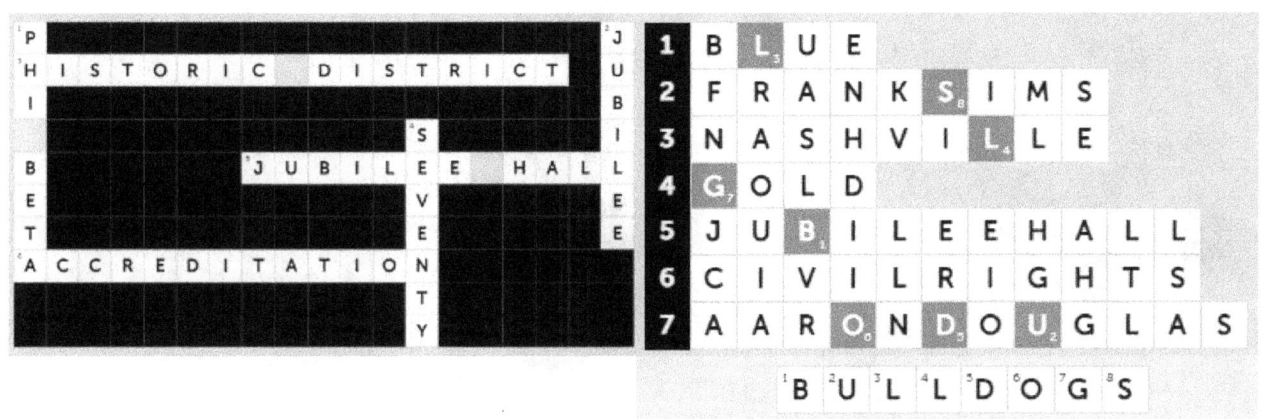

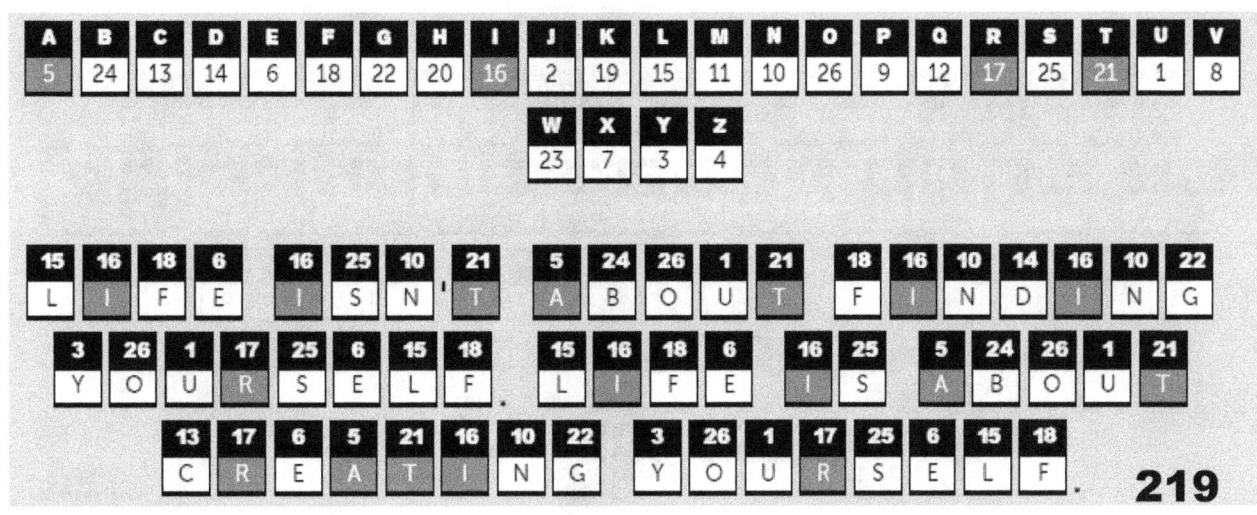

UMES
Answers

1. Which name came from a member of trustees?
   A. Princess Anne Academy
   B. Morgan College
   C. Maryland State College
2. What year UMES become an University?
   A. 1970
   B. 1948
   C. 1919
3. What was UMES original name?
   A. Maryland State College
   B. Princess Anne Academy
   C. Delaware Conference Academy

1. MAROON AND GRAY
2. PHARMACY
3. HAWKS
4. PRINCESS-ANNE
5. ARTSHELL
6. SPACEGRANT
7. HEIDI ANDERSON

DEEDS NOT WORDS

A	B	C	D	E	F	G	H	I	J	K	L	M	N	O	P	Q	R	S	T	U	V
20	7	12	19	10	8	26	15	17	1	6	16	13	18	4	11	5	14	24	25	21	22

W	X	Y	Z
3	2	9	23

THERE IS ALWAYS LIGHT IF WE'RE BRAVE ENOUGH TO SEE IT. THERE IS ALWAYS LIGHT IF WE'RE BRAVE ENOUGH TO BE IT.

220

Claflin University Answers

1. Who was Claflin University named after?
   A. Lee Claflin
   B. Alonzo Webster
   C. William Claflin
2. Claflin was the first college to do what in SC?
   A. Have an Medical department
   B. Accept all students regardless of race or gender
   C. Graduate a male and female
3. Claflin is the oldest HBCU in?
   A. North Carolina
   B. South Dakota
   C. South Carolina

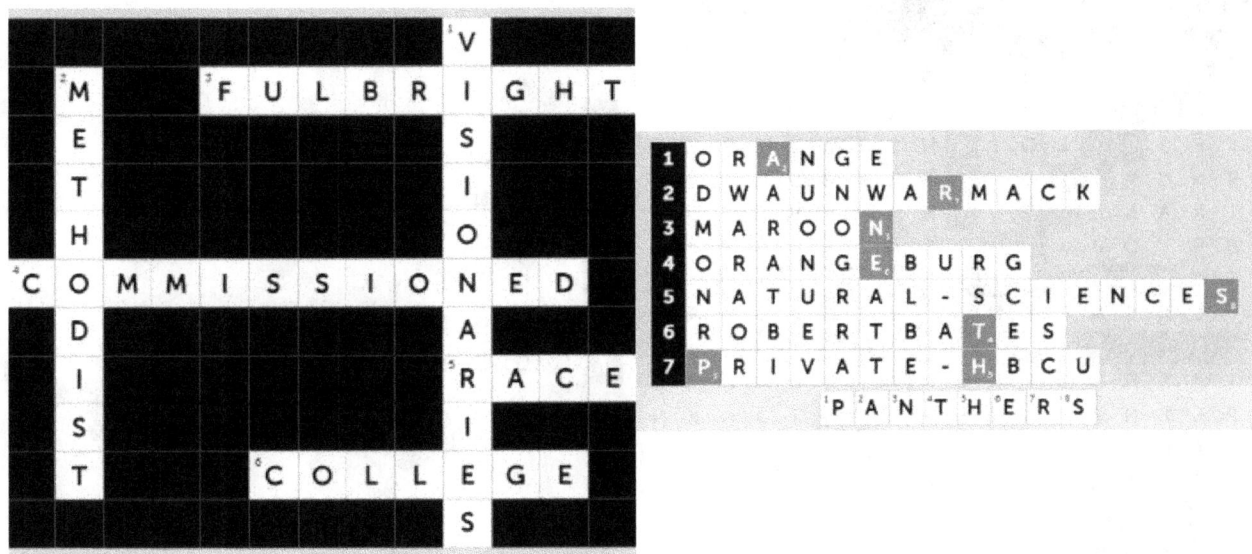

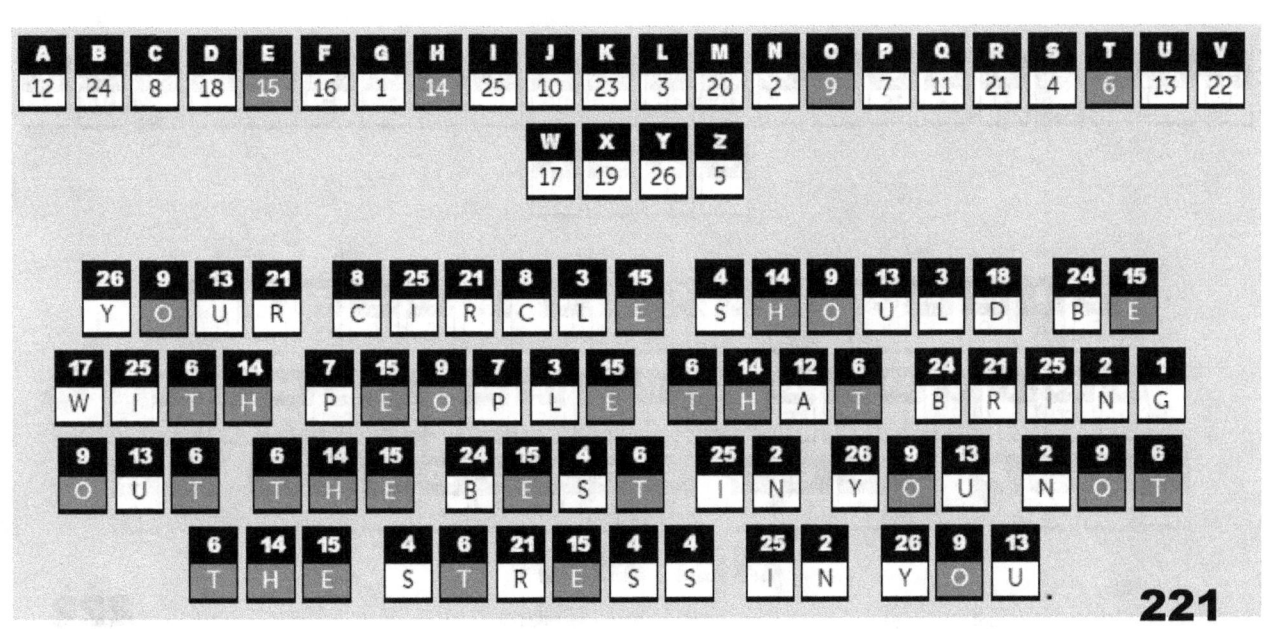

YOUR CIRCLE SHOULD BE WITH PEOPLE THAT BRING OUT THE BEST IN YOU NOT THE STRESS IN YOU.

221

WSSU Answers

1. Which name did WSSU start off with?
   A. Winston-Salem Teachers College
   B. Winston-Salem State College
   C. Slater Industrial Academy
2. What year did WSSC become a University?
   A. 1963
   B. 1969
   C. 1925
3. What was WSSU the first HBCU to do?
   A. Offer a Bachelors degree
   B. Offer specialized training
   C. Offer a Associates degree

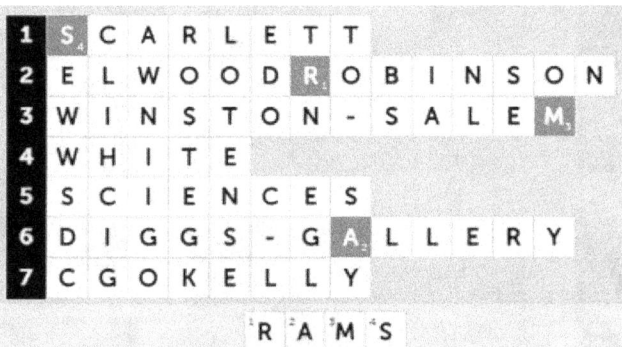

1. SCARLETT
2. ELWOOD ROBINSON
3. WINSTON-SALEM
4. WHITE
5. SCIENCES
6. DIGGS-GALLERY
7. CGOKELLY

RAMS

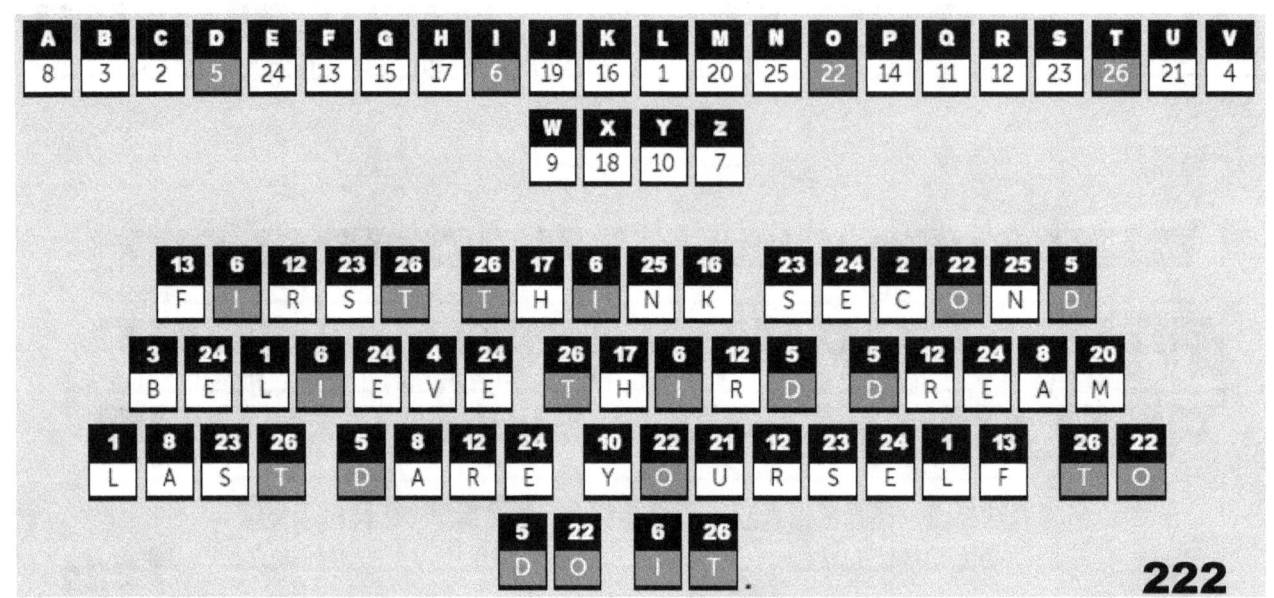

FIRST THINK SECOND BELIEVE THIRD DREAM LAST DARE YOURSELF TO DO IT.

222

DSU Answers

1. Which name was changed to stop confusion in the state?
   A. State College for Colored Students
   B. Delaware College
   C. Delaware College for Colored Students
2. What year DSU become an university?
   A. 1947
   B. 1993
   C. 1893
3. DSU was the first HBCU to do what?
   A. Acquire an land-grant from the state
   B. Acquire an HBCU
   C. Acquire an institution that is not a HBCU

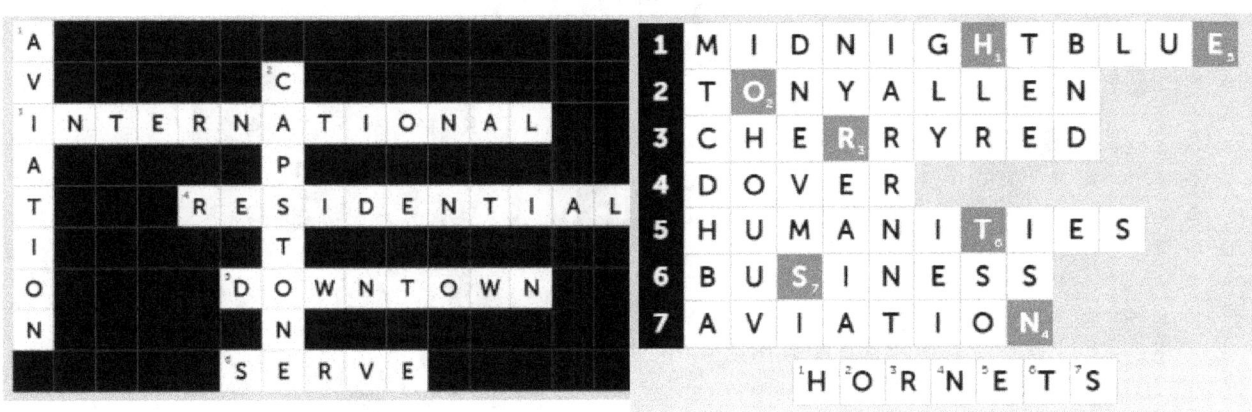

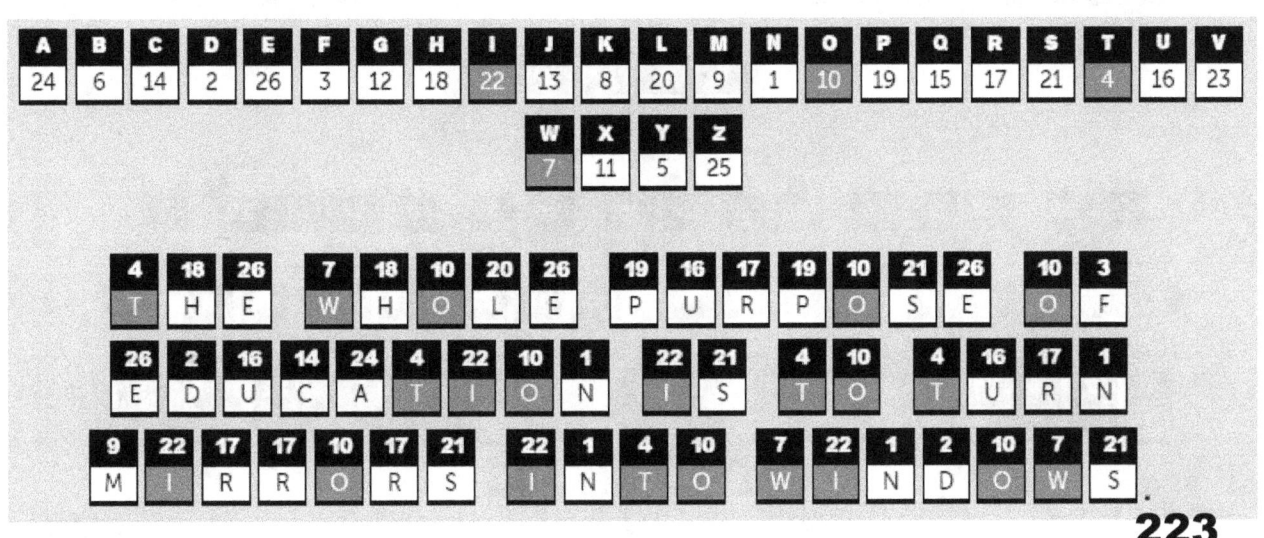

"THE WHOLE PURPOSE OF EDUCATION IS TO TURN MIRRORS INTO WINDOWS"

223

Tougaloo College Answers

1. Where was Tougaloo College founded at?
   A. Tougaloo, MS
   B. Jackson, MS
   C. Madison, MS
2. What year was Tougaloo College established?
   A. 1869
   B. 1861
   C. 1870
3. What is Tougaloo sometimes referred to as?
   A. Cradle of the graves in Mississippi
   B. Cradle of the Civil Rights Movement in Mississippi
   C. Cradle of humankind in Mississippi

1. ROYAL BLUE
2. CARMEN WALTERS
3. SCARLET
4. TOUGALOO-NINE
5. MISSISSIPPI
6. MEDGAR EVERS
7. COLLEGE FUND

BULLDOGS

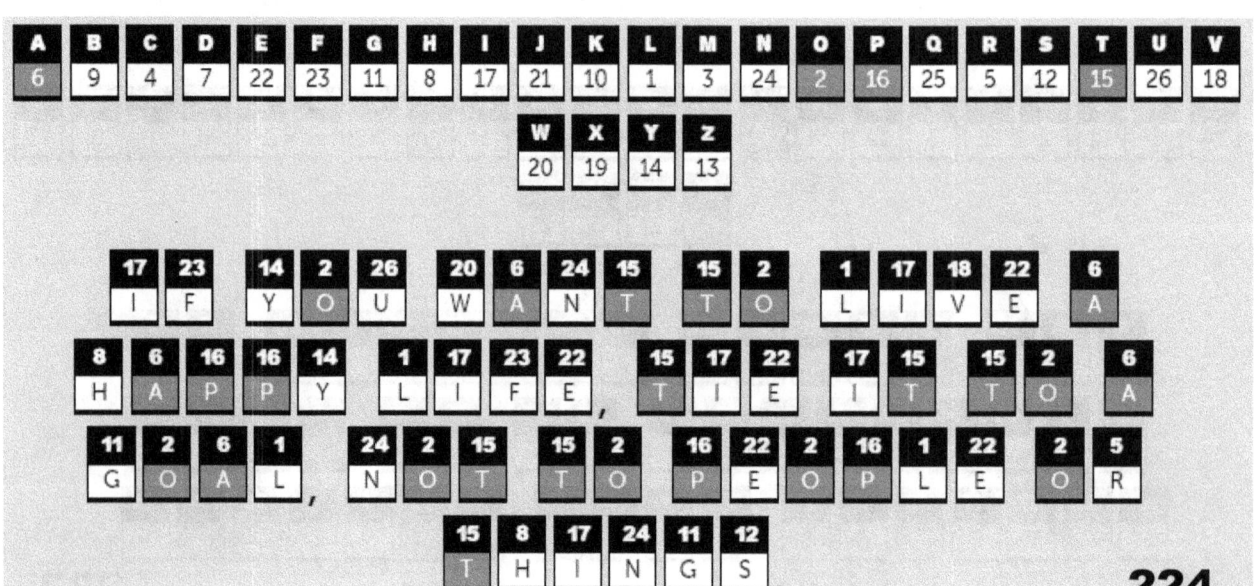

"IF YOU WANT TO LIVE A HAPPY LIFE, TIE IT TO A GOAL, NOT TO PEOPLE OR THINGS."

224

1. Where did the name for Morgan College come from?
   A. The State Assembly of Maryland
   B. Baltimore Conference of Methodist Episcopal Church
   C. In honor of the Reverend Lyttleton Morgan
2. What year did Morgan College become an University?
   A. 1937
   B. 1890
   C. 1975
3. What type of college did MSU start as?
   A. Research school
   B. Ministry school
   C. Medical school

MSU Answers

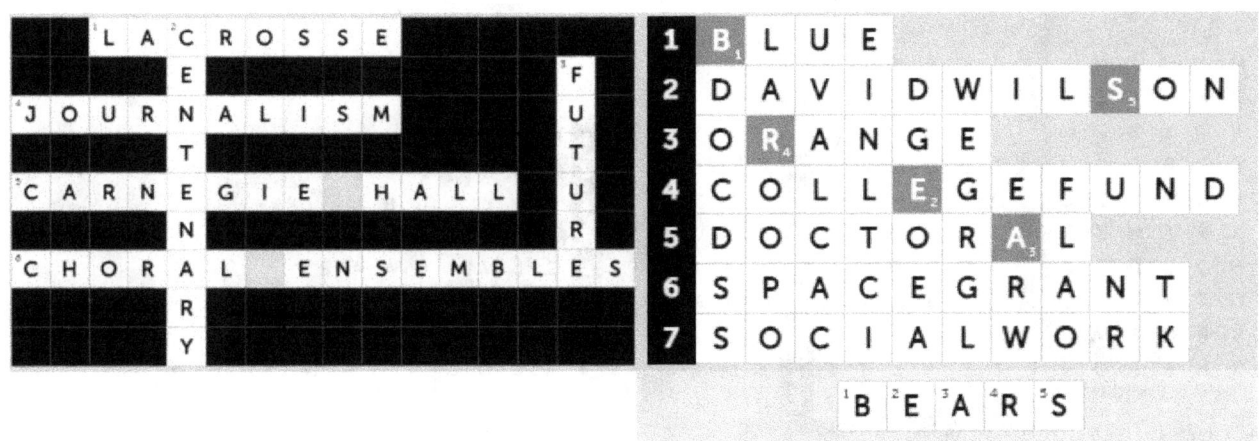

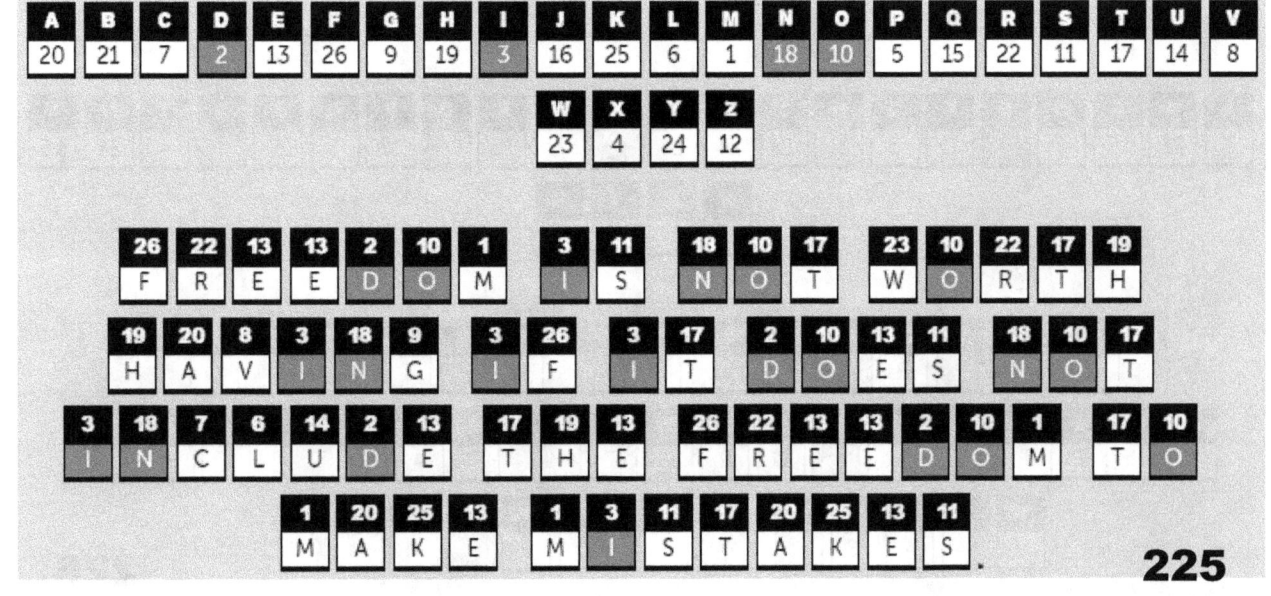

1. Which colleges merged to create Dillard University?
   A. Straight College
   B. New Orleans University
   C. University of Louisiana at Lafayette
2. What year did Dillard become an University?
   A. 1873
   B. 1934
   C. 1915
3. How did Dillard University get it's name?
   A. James H. Dillard
   B. United Church of Christ
   C. United Methodist Church

Dillard University
Answers

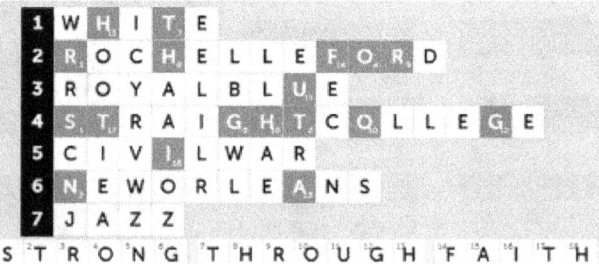

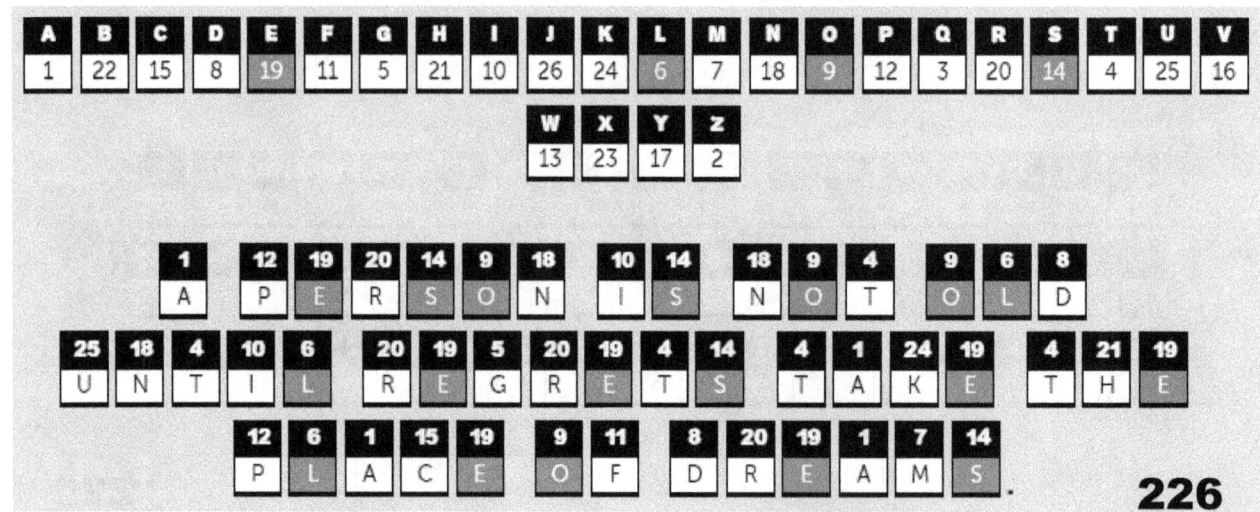

226

NCCU Answers

1. Who founded NC Central?
   A. Dr. James E. Shepard
   B. Margaret Olivia Slocum Sage
   C. American Missionary Association
2. What year did NCCU become an University?
   A. 1947
   B. 1969
   C. 1925
3. Why did our name get changed to NCCD ?
   A. They added a four-year curriculum
   B. They added graduate courses
   C. They got state funding

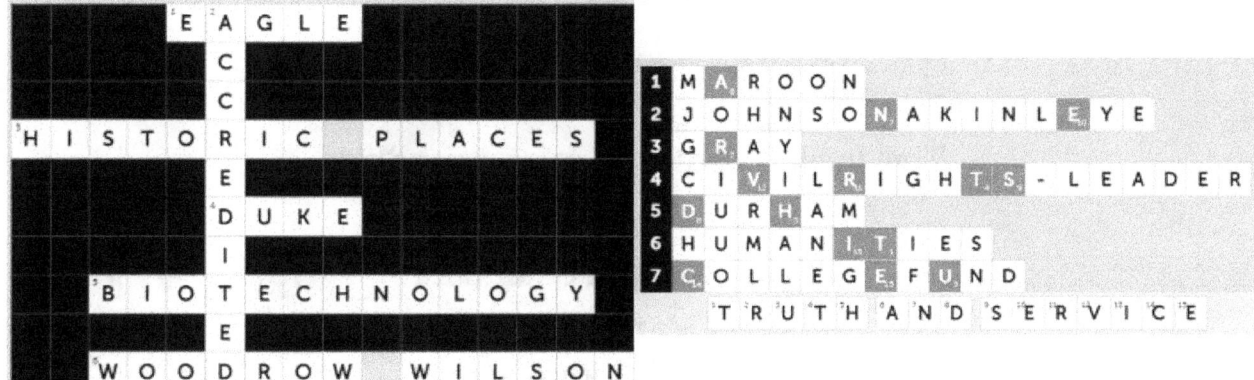

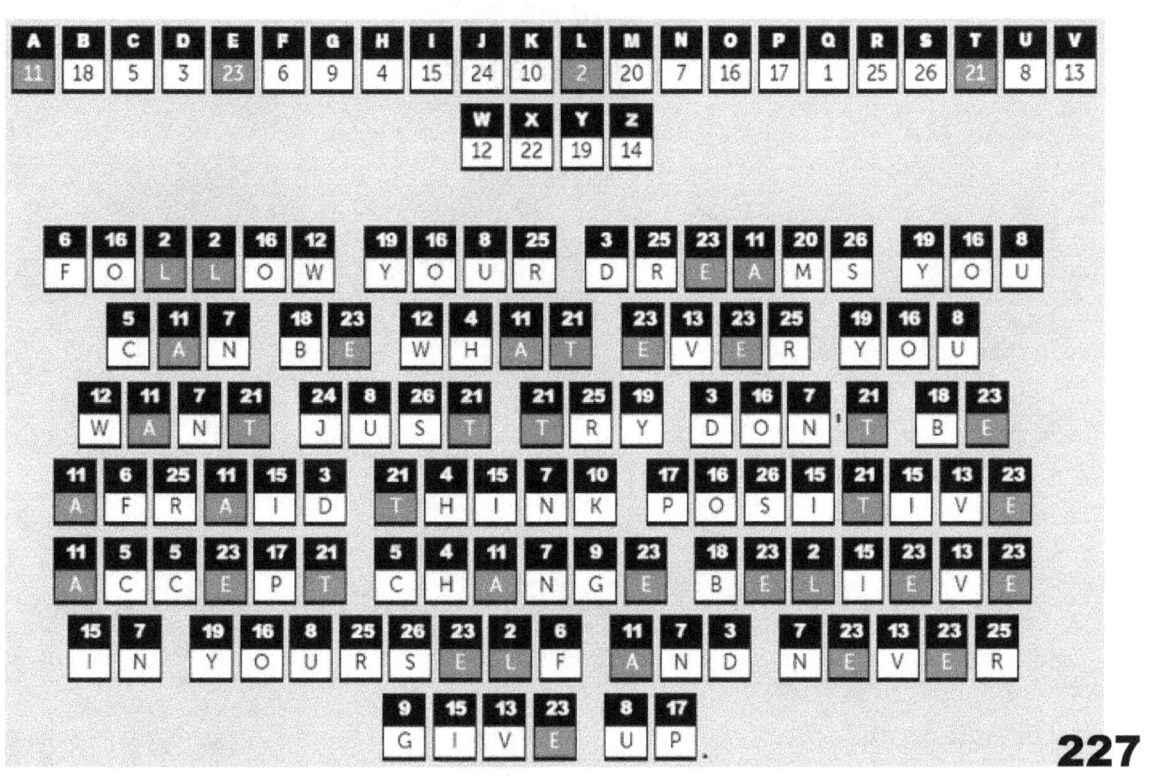

This book is dedicated to my grandkids
Anais Isabella Pablo-Antonio
Deyshawn Frank Chambers
Alicia Marie Jackson
Ayianna Marie Chambers
Zion Jamaris Jackson
Jayvon Jerome Jackson

ABOUT THE AUTHOR

Matthew D. Hale, the author of Black Historical Figures is a retired Marine and disabled veteran. He received his Bachelor of Arts in Computer Science from Campbell University and his Master of Science in Computer Engineering from Boston University. Matthew spends his down time making music, traveling, playing, and developing his own video games. Follow Matthew on Facebook/Meta at wegonnalearntoday, Instagram @ w_g_l_t and Tic Tok at wegonnalearntoday. Go to wegonnalearntoday.com or everydollarcountz.com for additional information.

In 2020 Matthew developed an interactive website, www.wegonnalearntoday, to provide access to Black History through games, music and videos. The website grew into the Black Historical Figures workbook series as a way to supplement the black history curricula taught in the school systems.

'In order to grow you must visit uncomfortable places'

10 BOOK SERIES
RELEASE DATES

NOVEMBER 2022

FEBRUARY 2023

MAY 2023

AUGUST 2023

NOVEMBER 2023

GET YOUR COPY TODAY
DON'T FORGET TO TELL A FRIEND

www.ingramcontent.com/pod-product-compliance
Lightning Source LLC
Chambersburg PA
CBHW080335170426
43194CB00014B/2569